FOLLOW YOUR DREAMS

ISBN: 978-1-300-81868-7

www.melanieyoung.net

I dedicate this book to my friend, Andy Spaschak, who always inspires me, either through his deep, poetic, philosophical thoughts or his amazing photographs.

If you're not living you're dying and it's nobody's fault but your own.

~Andy Spaschak

Follow Your Dreams

INSPIRATIONAL QUOTES

I have been 'collecting' inspirational quotes since 1975, I was eleven years old. I had quotes tucked in everywhere – and I know there are many I have missed that didn't make it into this book.

Just because a quote is in this book doesn't mean that I like or respect every person whose quotes are on these pages; and I don't necessarily agree with all of them either. Some of the quotes are inspirational, some are humorous, some are thought provoking, and some just make me want to get into a heated debate. Being a Christian, I often have to mentally insert God into the quote so that I may agree with it.

I hope you get as much from these quotes as I do!

Follow Your Dreams

"Everyone is your best friend when you are successful. Make sure that the people that you surround yourself with are also the people that you are not afraid of failing with."

~Paula Abdul

"Keep the faith, don't lose your perseverance and always trust your gut extinct."

~Paula Abdul

"Great necessities call out great virtues."

~Abigail Adams

"Learning is not attained by chance, it must be sought for with ardor and diligence."

~Abigail Adams

"We have too many high-sounding words, and too few actions that correspond with them."

~Abigail Adams

"Listen to your inner voice for it is a deep and powerful source of wisdom, beauty and truth, ever flowing through you.

Learn to trust it, trust your intuition, and in good time, answers to all you seek to know will come, and the path will open before you."

~Caroline Joy Adams

"Success has made failures of many men."

~Cindy Adams

"Human beings, who are almost unique in having the ability to learn from the experience of others, are also remarkable for their apparent disinclination to do so."
~Douglas Adams

"I love deadlines. I like the whooshing sound they make as they fly by."
~Douglas Adams

"Courage and perseverance have a magical talisman, before which difficulties disappear and obstacles vanish into air."
~John Quincy Adams

"If your actions inspire others to dream more, learn more, do more and become more, you are a leader."
~John Quincy Adams

"Old minds are like old horses; you must exercise them if you wish to keep them in working order."
~John Adams

"There are two educations. One should teach us how to make a living and the other how to live."
~John Adams

"If your actions inspire others to dream more, learn more, do more and become more, you are a leader."
~John Quincy Adams

"Patience and perseverance have a magical effect before which difficulties disappear and obstacles vanish. A little knowledge that acts is worth infinitely more than much knowledge that is idle."
~John Quincy Adams

"Cheerfulness is the best promoter of health and is as friendly to the mind as to the body."
~Joseph Addison

"I'm not afraid of storms, for I'm learning to sail my ship."
~Aeschylus

"Of prosperity mortals can never have enough."
~Aeschylus

"Please all, and you will please none."
~Aesop

"Nobody will think you're somebody if you don't think so yourself."
~African-American Proverb

"When elephants fight it is the grass that suffers."
~African saying

"As you grow, you learn more. If you stayed as ignorant as you were at twenty-two, you'd always be twenty-two. Aging is not just decay, you know. It's growth. It's more than the negative that you're going to die, it's the positive that you understand you're going to die, and that you live a better life because of it."
~Mitch Albom

"It's not just other people we need to forgive. We also need to forgive ourselves. For all the things we didn't do. All the things we should have done."
~Mitch Albom

"I'm not afraid of storms, for I am learning how to sail my ship."
~Louisa May Alcott

"We all have our own life to pursue, our own kind of dream to be weaving. And we all have some power to make wishes come true, as long as we keep believing."

~Louisa May Alcott

"Begin challenging your own assumptions. Your assumptions are your windows on the world. Scrub them off every once in awhile, or the light won't come in."

~Alan Alda

"Age is whatever you think it is. You are as old as you think you are."

~Muhammad Ali

"I am the astronaut of boxing. Joe Louis and Dempsey were just jet pilots. I'm in a world of my own."
~Muhammad Ali

"I hated every minute of training, but I said, 'Don't quit. Suffer now and live the rest of your life as a champion.'"
~Muhammad Ali

"If they can make penicillin out of moldy bread, they can sure make something out of you."

~Muhammad Ali

"To be a great champion you must believe you are the best. If you're not, pretend you are."
~Muhammad Ali

"The world is a grindstone and life is your nose."

~Fred Allen

"Each of us has been put on earth with the ability to do something well. We cheat ourselves and the world if we don't use that ability as best we can."

~Gracie Allen

"Circumstance does not make the man; it reveals him to himself."

~James Allen

"For true success ask yourself these four questions: Why? Why not? Why not me? Why not now?"
~James Allen

"Your vision is the promise of what you shall one day be; your ideal is the prophecy of what you shall at last unveil."

~James Allen

"Be strong enough to stand alone, be yourself enough to stand apart, but be wise enough to stand together when the time comes."
~Mark Amend

"Don't count every day of the week; make every day of the week count."

~Mark Amend

"Sometimes opportunities float right past your nose. Work hard, apply yourself, and be ready. When an opportunity comes you can grab it."

~Julie Andrews

"No one is in control of your happiness but you; therefore, you have the power to change anything about yourself or your life that you want to change."

~Barbara de Angelis

"Cooking is like writing poetry, be careful in the choice of your ingredients and respectful of how they work together. That's true of all the efforts in life."

~Maya Angelou

"I believe that every person is born with talent."
~Maya Angelou

"I can be changed by what happens to me, but i refuse to be reduced by it."
~Maya Angelou

"Life is not measured by the number of breaths we take, but by the moments that take our breath away."

~Maya Angelou

"Nothing will work unless you do."

~Maya Angelou

"Perhaps travel cannot prevent bigotry, but by demonstrating that all people cry, laugh, eat, worry, and die, it can introduce the idea that if we try and understand each other, we may even become friends."

~Maya Angelou

"Success is liking yourself, liking what you do, and liking how you do it."

~Maya Angelou

"We delight in the beauty of the butterfly, but rarely admit the changes it has gone through to achieve that beauty."

~Maya Angelou

"You may not control all the events that happen to you, but you can decide not to be reduced by them."

~Maya Angelou

"The greater your capacity to love, the greater your capacity to feel the pain."

~Jennifer Aniston

"Love is, above all, the gift of oneself."

~Jean Anouilh

"Now and then it's good to pause in our pursuit of happiness and just be happy."
~Guillaume Apollinaire

"Here's to the crazy ones. The misfits. The rebels. The troublemakers. The round pegs in the square holes. The ones who see things differently. They're not fond of rules. And they have no respect for the status quo. You can quote them, disagree with them, glorify or vilify them. About the only thing you can't do is ignore them. Because they change things.

They push the human race forward. And while some may see them as the crazy ones, we see genius. Because the people who are crazy enough to think they can change the world, are the ones who do."

~Apple Inc.

"I don't want to give any advice to a 19-year-old, because I want a 19-year-old to make mistakes and learn from them. Make mistakes, make mistakes, make mistakes. Just make sure they're your mistakes."

~Fiona Apple

"When you're always trying to conform to the norm, you lose your uniqueness, which can be the foundation for your greatness."

~Dale Archer

"It is the mark of an educated mind to be able to entertain a thought without accepting it."
~Aristotle

"Knowing what is right does not make sagacious man."

~Aristotle

"Love is composed of a single soul inhabiting two bodies."

~Aristotle

"Pleasure in the job puts perfection in the work."

~Aristotle

"Pain is temporary. It may last a minute, or an hour, or a day, or a year, but eventually it will subside and something else will take its place. If I quit, however, it lasts forever."

~Lance Armstrong

"Aerodynamically, the bumble bee shouldn't be able to fly, but the bumble bee doesn't know it so it goes on flying anyway."

~Mary Kay Ash

"The only difference between successful people and unsuccessful people is extraordinary determination."

~Mary Kay Ash

"You've got to get to the stage in life where going for it is more important than winning or losing."
~Arthur Ashe

"In the end, vision, drive, energy, singleness of purpose, wise use of resources, and a commitment to a destiny worthy of his efforts become a character of a chieftain who excels."

~Attila the Hun

"Accept the things to which fate binds you, and love the people with whom fate brings you together, but do so with all your heart."

~Marcus Aelius Aurelius

"Look within. Within is the fountain of good, and it will ever bubble up, if thou wilt ever dig."

~Marcus Aurelius

"Your life is what your thoughts make it."
~Marcus Aurelius

"Man learns through experience, and the spiritual path is full of different kinds of experiences. He will encounter many difficulties and obstacles, and they are the very experiences he needs to encourage and complete the cleansing process."
~Sai Baba

"A wise man will make more opportunities than he finds."
~Francis Bacon

"They know enough who know how to learn."
~Francis Bacon

"What the world really needs is more love and less paper work."
~Pearl Bailey

"Man imposes his own limitations, don't set any."
~Anthony Baily

"Ability is of little account without opportunity."
~Lucille Ball

"Love yourself first and everything else falls into line. You really have to love yourself to get anything done in this world."
~Lucille Ball

Admit to -- and learn from -- your mistakes. Mistakes must be viewed positively... because with the knowledge you gain from them, you are able to do better in the future. So much can be accomplished with a long-term vision and resilience to short-term setbacks. Not every problem is conquered overnight, but if you persist and never give in to your mistakes, you will succeed.

~Craig Ballantyne

"It is always the simple that produces the marvelous."

~Amelia Barr

"Let no one who loves be unhappy, even love unreturned has its rainbow."

~James M. Barrie

"Nothing is really work unless you would rather be doing something else."

~James M. Barrie

"All of us are born with a set of instinctive fears - of falling, of the dark, of lobsters, of falling on lobsters in the dark, or speaking before a Rotary Club, and of the words, Some Assembly Required."

~Dave Barry

"Life is anything that dies when you stomp on it."

~Dave Barry

"I think happiness is what makes you pretty. Period. Happy people are beautiful. They become like a mirror and they reflect that happiness."

~Drew Barrymore

"A man is not old until regrets take the place of dreams."
~John Barrymore

"Gratitude unlocks the fullness of life. It turns what we have into enough, and more. It turns denial into acceptance, chaos to order, confusion to clarity. It can turn a meal into a feast, a house into a home, a stranger into a friend. Gratitude makes sense of our past, brings peace for today, and creates a vision for tomorrow."

~Melody Beattie

"Steve Jobs, Albert Einstein, Thomas Edison, Benjamin Franklin. All people who poured all their creative and scientific energy into changing the world, not protesting it. Don't waste time Occupying Wall Street. Occupy your life. Change the world."

~Glenn Beck

"Daring to have a wonderful experience, even though you may get hurt, is the only way you'll realize its deepest desires."

~Martha Beck

"Just one mental shift -- focusing on the abundance of your environment-- switches your psychological settings so that your life automatically improves in many areas you may think are unrelated. This is essentially a leap from fear to faith."

~Martha Beck

"I believe that you're great, that there's something magnificent about you. Regardless of what has happened to you in your life, regardless of how young or how old you think you might be, the moment you begin to think properly, there's something that is within you, there's power within you, that's greater than the world. It will begin to emerge. It will take over your life. It will feed you. It will clothe you. It will guide you, protect you, direct you, sustain your very existence, if you let it. Now, that is what I know for sure."

~Michael Beckwith

"It is not what we take up, but what we give up, that makes us rich."
~Henry Ward Beecher

"Men's best successes come after their disappointments."
~Henry Ward Beecher

"We never know the love of a parent till we become parents ourselves."
~Henry Ward Beecher

"Any change, even a change for the better, is always accompanied by drawbacks and discomforts."
~Arnold Bennett

"As sure as the spring will follow the winter, prosperity and economic growth will follow recession."
~Bo Bennett

"Happiness is good health and a bad memory."
~Ingrid Bergman

"If opportunity doesn't knock, build a door."
~Milton Berle

"Our attitudes control our lives. Attitudes are a secret power working twenty-four hours a day, for good or bad. It is of paramount importance that we know how to harness and control this great force."
~Irving Berlin

"Focus on the present, and enhance your time and life now rather than always working toward tomorrow."
~Dr. Laura Berman

"If the world was perfect, it wouldn't be."
~Yogi Berra

"You've got to be very careful if you don't know where you are going, because you might not get there."

~Yogi Berra

"The bird of paradise alights only on the hand that does not grasp."

~John Berry

"Blessed are those who can give without remembering and take without forgetting."

~Elizabeth Bibesco

"Life consists not in holding good cards but in playing those you hold well."

~Josh Billings

"Silence is one of the hardest arguments to refute."

~Josh Billings

"Leadership is getting players to believe in you. If you tell a teammate you're ready to play as tough as you're able to, you'd better go out there and do it. Players will see right through a phony. And they can tell when you're not giving it all you've got."

~Larry Bird

"Life consists not in holding good cards but in playing those you hold well."

~Josh Billings

"Confidence sells -- people believe in those who believe in themselves. No one wants to be stuck in a room with other people who feel like they don't deserve to be there. Stop wondering if you're good enough. Know you are, and start acting like it."

~Simon Black

"The six W's: Work will win when wishing won't."

~Todd Blackledge

"The thankful receiver bears a plentiful harvest."

~William Blake

"If you have something to do that is worthwhile doing, don't talk about it, but do it. After you have done it, your friends and enemies will talk about it."

~George W. Blount

"All of us have moments in our lives that test our courage. Taking children into a house with a white carpet is one of them."

~Erma Bombeck

"A throne is only a bench covered with velvet."

~Napoleon Bonaparte

"Glory is fleeting, but obscurity is forever."

~Napoleon Bonaparte

"Imagination rules the world."

~Napoleon Bonaparte

"To be one, to be united is a great thing. But to respect the right to be different is maybe even greater."
~Bono

"Dreams are the seeds of change. Nothing ever grows without a seed, and nothing ever changes without a dream."

~Debby Boone

"If you take a deep breath and look around, 'Look what's happening to me!' can become 'Look what's happening!' And what's happening? The incredible drama of life is happening. And we're in it!"

~Sylvia Boorstein

"Freedom means the opportunity to be what we never thought we would be."

~Daniel J. Boorstin

"Don't think. Thinking is the enemy of creativity. It's self-conscious, and anything self-conscious is lousy. You can't try to do things. You simply must do things."

~Ray Bradbury

"If we had no winter, the spring would not be so pleasant: if we did not sometimes taste of adversity, prosperity would not be so welcome."

~Anne Bradstreet

"Don't tell me the sky's the limit when there are footprints on the moon."

~Paul Brandt

"Whoever you are, there is some younger person who thinks you are perfect. There is some work that will never be done if you don't do it. There is someone who would miss you if you were gone. There is a place that you alone can fill."

~Jacob Braude

"Life is a brief opportunity to do something prehumously."

~Robert Brault

"Why you? Because there's no one better. Why now? Because tomorrow isn't soon enough."

~Donna Brazile

"Love is when you meet someone who tells you something new about yourself."

~Andre Breton

"A successful person is one who can lay a firm foundation with the bricks that others throw at him or her."
~David Brinkley

"I try to avoid looking forward or backward, and try to keep looking upward."
~Charlotte Bronte

"Life appears to me too short to be spent in nursing animosity or registering wrongs."
~Charlotte Bronte

"A kiss makes the heart young again and wipes out the years."
~Rupert Brooke

"Look, I don't want to wax philosophic, but I will say that if you're alive you've got to flap your arms and legs, you've got to jump around a lot, for life is the very opposite of death, and therefore you must at very least think noisy and colorfully, or you're not alive."
~Mel Brooks

"Success is a state of mind. If you want success, start thinking of yourself as a success."
~Dr. Joyce Brothers

"Belonging starts with self-acceptance ... Believing that you're enough is what gives you the courage to be authentic."
~Brene Brown

"Don't say you don't have enough time. You have exactly the same number of hours per day that were given to Helen Keller, Pasteur, Michelangelo, Mother Teresa, Leonardo da Vinci, Thomas Jefferson, and Albert Einstein."
~H. Jackson Brown Jr.

"The best preparation for tomorrow is doing your best today."

~H. Jackson Brown, Jr.

"You are where you are today because you've chosen to be there."

~Harry Browne

"Do not get angry because others question what you believe, be calm and loving, for anger is the root of a faulty belief."

~Leon Brown

"Accept responsibility for your life. Know that it is you who will get you where you want to go, no one else."

~Les Brown

"Never let someone's opinion become your reality. Never sacrifice who you are because someone else has a problem with it. Love who you are inside and out."

~Les Brown

"Light tomorrow with today."

~Elizabeth Barrett Browning

"If you believe in yourself and have dedication and pride - and never quit, you'll be a winner. The price of victory is high but so are the rewards."
~Paul Bryant

"True friends are those who really know you but love you anyway."

~Edna Buchanan

"I don't wait for moods. You accomplish nothing if you do that. Your mind must know it has got to get down to work."

~Pearl S. Buck

"Love dies only when growth stops."
~Pearl S. Buck

"An insincere and evil friend is more to be feared than a wild beast; a wild beast may wound your body, but an evil friend will wound your mind."
~Buddha

"It is better to travel well than to arrive."
~Buddha

"There are two mistakes one can make along the road to truth - not going all the way, and not starting. "
~Buddha

"Thousands of candles can be lit from a single candle, and the life of the candle will not be shortened. Happiness never decreases by being shared."
~Buddha

"Chains of habit are too light to be felt until they are too heavy to be broken."
~Warren Buffett

"In the business world, the rearview mirror is always clearer than the windshield."
~Warren Buffett

"We learn to walk by stumbling."
~Bulgarian Proverb

"Be yourself, take control of your life."
~Emma Bunton

"We must all obey the great law of change. It is the most powerful law of nature."

~Edmund Burke

"I'd rather be a failure at something I enjoy than be a success at something I hate."
~George Burns

"One resolution I have made, and try always to keep, is this:

To rise above the little things."

~John Burroughs

"Your mind will answer most questions if you learn to relax and wait for the answer."

~William S. Burroughs

"Love is life. And if you miss love, you miss life."
~ Leo Buscaglia

"Never idealize others. They will never live up to your expectations. Don't over-analyze your relationships. Stop playing games. A growing relationship can only be nurtured by genuineness."

~Leo Buscaglia

"The fact that I can plant a seed and it becomes a flower, share a bit of knowledge and it becomes another's, smile at someone and receive a smile in return, are to me continual spiritual exercises."

~Leo Buscaglia

"The easiest thing to be in the world is you. The most difficult thing to be is what other people want you to be."

~Leo Buscaglia

"We will not tire, we will not falter and we will not fail."
~George W. Bush, in response to the attacks on September 11, 2001

"I do not know the word 'quit.' Either I never did, or I have abolished it."
~Susan Butcher

"You can be the most beautiful person in the world and everybody sees light and rainbows when they look at you, but if you yourself don't know it, all of that doesn't even matter. Every second that you spend on doubting your worth, every moment that you use to criticize yourself, is a second of your life wasted, is a moment of your life thrown away. It's not like you have forever, so don't waste any of your seconds, don't throw even one of your moments away."

~C. JoyBell C.

"A man begins cutting his wisdom teeth the first time he bites off more than he can chew."

~Herb Caen

"Be like a duck. Calm on the surface, but always paddling like the dickens underneath."

~Michael Caine

"When we are dreaming alone it is only a dream. When we are dreaming with others, it is the beginning of reality."

~Dom Helder Camara

"People who have only good experiences aren't very interesting. They may be content, and happy after a fashion, but they aren't very deep. It may seem a misfortune now, and it makes things difficult, but well -- it's easy to feel all the happy, simple stuff. Not that happiness is necessarily simple. But I don't think you're going to have a life like that, and I think you'll be the better for it. The difficult thing is to not be overwhelmed by the bad patches. You must not let them defeat you. You must see them as a gift -- a cruel gift, but a gift nonetheless."
~Peter Cameron

"Love is a friendship set to music."

~Joseph Campbell

"We must be willing to let go of the life we planned in order to have the life that is waiting for us."

~Joseph Campbell

"Every time you take a risk or move out of your comfort zone, you have a great opportunity to learn more about yourself and your capacity."

~Jack Canfield

"There are only two words that will always lead you to success. Those words are yes and no. Undoubtedly, you've mastered saying yes. So start practicing saying no. Your goals depend on it!"

~Jack Canfield

"Strong feelings do not necessarily make a strong character. The strength of a man is to be measured by the power of the feelings he subdues not by the power of those which subdue him."

~William Carleton

"A loving heart is the beginning of all knowledge."

~Thomas Carlyle

"And while the law of competition may be sometimes hard for the individual, it is best for the race, because it ensures the survival of the fittest in every department."
~Andrew Carnegie

"Those who contemplate the beauty of the earth find reserves of strength that will endure as long as life lasts. There is something infinitely healing in the repeated refrains of nature -- the assurance that dawn comes after night, and spring after winter."

~Rachel Carson

"You must accept that you might fail; then, if you do your best and still don't win, at least you can be satisfied that you've tried. If you don't accept failure as a possibility, you don't set high goals, you don't branch out, you don't try - you don't take the risk."

~Rosalynn Carter

"You build on failure. You use it as a stepping stone. Close the door on the past. You don't try to forget the mistakes, but you don't dwell on it. You don't let it have any of your energy, or any of your time, or any of your space."

~Johnny Cash

"Every year of my life I grow more convinced that it is wisest and best to fix our attention on the beautiful and the good, and dwell as little as possible on the evil and the false."
~Richard Cecil

"The most wasted day of all is that during which we have not laughed."

~Sebastian R. N. Chamfort

"Opportunity does not knock, it presents itself when you beat down the door."
~Kyle Chandler

"Never does the human soul appear so strong as when it foregoes revenge and dares to forgive an injury."

~Edwin Hubbel Chapin

"A day without laughter is a day wasted."

~Charles Chaplin

"Avoid the crowd. Do your own thinking independently. Be the chess player, not the chess piece."

~Ralph Charell

"Don't rely on someone else for your happiness and self worth. Only you can be responsible for that. If you can't love and respect yourself - no one else will be able to make that happen. Accept who you are - completely; the good and the bad - and make changes as YOU see fit - not because you think someone else wants you to be different."

~Stacey Charter

"Life can be like a roller coaster. And just when you think you've had enough, and you're ready to get off the ride and take the calm, easy merry-go round, you change your mind, throw your hands in the air and ride the roller coaster all over again. That's exhilaration... that's living a bit on the edge... that's being alive."

~Stacey Charter

"Life is all about timing... the unreachable becomes reachable, the unavailable become available, the unattainable... attainable. Have the patience, wait it out. It's all about timing."

~Stacey Charter

"Life is filled with so many exciting twists and turns. Hop off the straight and narrow whenever you can and take the winding paths. Experience the exhilaration of the view from the edge. Because the moments spent there, that take your breath away, are what make you feel truly alive."

~Stacey Charter

"Success builds character. Failure reveals it."

~Dave Checketts

"If we learn to open our hearts, anyone, including the people who drive us crazy, can be our teacher."

~Pema Chedron

"Everything in life comes to you as a teacher. Pay attention.

Learn quickly."

~Cherokee Saying

"Fairy tales are more than true; not because they tell us that dragons exist, but because they tell us that dragons can be beaten."

~G.K. Chesterton

"Courage is almost a contradiction in terms. It means a strong desire to live taking the form of readiness to die."

~G.K. Chesterton

"The way to love anything is to realize that it may be lost."

~Gilbert K. Chesterton

"The crime of loving is forgetting."

~Maurice Chevalier

"Find something you're passionate about and keep tremendously interested in it."

~Julia Child

"Belief in oneself is one of the most important bricks in building any successful venture."

~Lydia M. Child

"The miracle is not to fly in the air, or to walk on the water, but to walk on the earth."

~Chinese Proverb

"When I let go of what I am, I become what I might be. When I let go of what I have, I receive what I need."

~Tao Te Ching

"A pessimist sees the difficulty in every opportunity; an optimist sees the opportunity in every difficulty."

~Winston Churchill

"Courage is rightly esteemed the first of human qualities... because it is the quality which guarantees all others."
~Winston Churchill

"Courage is what it takes to stand up and speak; courage is also what it takes to sit down and listen."
~Winston Churchill

"Kites rise highest against the wind, not with it."

~Winston Churchill

"Tact is the ability to tell someone to go to hell in such a way that they look forward to the trip."
~Winston S. Churchill

"To improve is to change; to be perfect is to change often."

~Winston Churchill

"We make a living by what we get, but we make a life by what we give."

~Winston Churchill

"When I look back on all these worries, I remember the story of the old man who said on his deathbed that he had had a lot of trouble in his life, most of which had never happened."

~Winston Churchill

"A man of courage is also full of faith."

~Cicero

"Every stage of human life, except the last, is marked out by certain and defined limits; old age alone has no precise and determinate boundary."

~Cicero

"Nothing is more noble, nothing more venerable than fidelity.

Faithfulness and truth are the most sacred excellences and endowments of the human mind."

~Cicero

"The only way to discover the limits of the possible is to go beyond them into the impossible."

~Arthur C. Clark

"A baby is born with a need to be loved – and never outgrows it."

~Frank Howard Clark

"The price of hating other human beings is loving oneself less."
~Eldridge Cleaver

"I would rather the man who presents something for my consideration subject me to a zephyr of truth and a gentle breeze of responsibility rather than blow me down with a curtain of hot wind."

~Grover Cleveland

"If you live long enough, you'll make mistakes. But if you learn from them, you'll be a better person. It's how you handle adversity, not how it affects you. The main thing is never quit, never quit, never quit."

~Bill Clinton

"I love, and the world is mine."

~Florence Earle Coates

"One is loved because one is loved. No reason is needed for loving."

~Paulo Coelho

"Really important meetings are planned by the souls long before the bodies see each other."

~Paulo Coelho

"Remember that wherever your heart is, there you will find your treasure."
~Paulo Coelho

"We need to forget what we think we are, so that we can really become what we are."
~Paulo Coelho

"When we love, we always strive to become better than we are. When we strive to become better than we are, everything around us becomes better too."
~Paulo Coelho

"When we strive to become better than we are, everything around us becomes better too."
~Paulo Coelho

"Follow your dreams, work hard, practice and persevere. Make sure you eat a variety of foods, get plenty of exercise and maintain a healthy lifestyle."
Sasha Cohen

"I've seen a baby cry then seconds later she laughed; the beauty of life, the pain never lasts."
~J. Cole

"A first love always remains in a secret place in the heart."
~Lamar Cole

"If a man is not rising upwards to be an angel, depend upon it, he is sinking downwards to be a devil."
~Samuel Taylor Coleridge

Follow Your Dreams

"You can do anything you wish to do, have anything you wish to have, be anything you wish to be."
~Robert Collier

"Success doesn't come to you, you go to it."
~Marva Collins

"Silence is foolish if we are wise, but wise if we are foolish."
~Charles Caleb Colton

"People will accept your ideas much more readily if you tell them Benjamin Franklin said it first."
~David H. Comins

"Behold the turtle. He makes progress only when he sticks his neck out."
~James Bryant Conant

"A journey of a thousand miles begins with a single step."
~Confucius

"Choose a job you love, and you will never have to work a day in your life."
~Confucius

"Everything has beauty, but not everyone sees it."
~Confucius

"If what one has to say is not better than silence, then one should keep silent."
~Confucius

"It is not the failure of others to appreciate your abilities that should trouble you, but rather your failure to appreciate theirs."
~Confucius

"The will to win, the desire to succeed, the urge to reach your full potential... these are the keys that will unlock the door to personal excellence."
~Confucius

"There is nothing like a challenge to bring out the best in man."
~Sean Connery

"Nothing can take the place of persistence."
~Calvin Coolidge

"All greatness of character is dependent on individuality."
~James F. Cooper

"I'm very proud of my flops, as much as of my successes."
~Francis Ford Coppola

"I don't know the key to success, but the key to failure is trying to please everyone."
~Bill Cosby

"People can be more forgiving than you can imagine. But you have to forgive yourself. Let go of what's bitter and move on."
~Bill Cosby

"If you want to test your memory, try to recall what you were worrying about one year ago today."
~E. Joseph Cossman

"Obstacles are things a person sees when he takes his eyes off his goal."
~E. Joseph Cossman

"Failure doesn't kill you... it increases your desire to make something happen."

~Kevin Costner

"You have to decide if you're going to wilt like a daisy or if you're just going to go forward and live the life that you've been granted."

~Kevin Costner

"Be fearless. Have the courage to take risks. Go where there are no guarantees. Get out of your comfort zone even if it means being uncomfortable. The road less traveled is sometimes fraught with barricades bumps and uncharted terrain. But it is on that road where your character is truly tested. And have the courage to accept that you're not perfect, nothing is and no one is -- and that's OK."

~Katie Couric

"If something comes to life in others because of you, then you have made an approach to immortality."

~Norman Cousins

"It takes generosity to discover the whole through others. If you realize you are only a violin, you can open yourself up to the world by playing your role in the concert."

~Jacques Yves Cousteau

"Effective leadership is putting first things first. Effective management is discipline, carrying it out."
~Stephen Covey

"Live out of your imagination not your history."

~Stephen R. Covey

"You have to decide what your highest priorities are and have the courage - pleasantly, smilingly, nonapologetically - to say no to other things. And the way to do that is by having a bigger yes burning inside."

~Stephen Covey

"If you must have motivation, think of your paycheck on Friday."
~Noel Coward

"A lot of life is dealing with your curse, dealing with the cards you were given that aren't so nice. Does it make you into a monster, or can you temper it in some way, or accept it and go in some other direction?"
~Wes Craven

"If you dig it, do it. If you dig it a lot, do it twice."
~Jim Croce

"He who stops being better stops being good."
~Oliver Cromwell

"I imagine that yes is the only living thing."
~E.E. Cummings

"Love is shown in your deeds, not in your words."
~Fr. Jerome Cummings

"Be less curious about people and more curious about ideas."
~Marie Curie

"I can never see what has been done; I only see what remains to be done."
~Marie Curie

"Nothing in life is to be feared. It is only to be understood. Now is the time to understand more, so that we may fear less."
~Marie Curie

"The only difference between me and a madman is that I'm not mad."
~Salvador Dali

"Become a student of change. It is the only thing that will remain constant."

~Anthony J. D'Angelo

"A man who dares to waste one hour of time has not discovered the value of life."
~Charles Darwin

"Do not fear mistakes – there are none."

~Miles Davis

"The energy spent trying to get revenge can be better spent creating an amazing life. Forget about them. Remember you."

~Thema Davis

"I have been impressed with the urgency of doing. Knowing is not enough; we must apply. Being willing is not enough; we must do."

~Leonardo da Vinci

"It had long since come to my attention that people of accomplishment rarely sat back and let things happen to them. They went out and happened to things."

~Leonardo da Vinci

"Life is pretty simple: You do some stuff. Most fails. Some works. You do more of what works. If it works big, others quickly copy it. Then you do something else. The trick is the doing something else."

~Leonardo da Vinci

"A sure way to lose happiness, I found, is to want it at the expense of everything else."
~Bette Davis

"You are good enough, smart enough, beautiful enough, strong enough. Believe it and stop letting insecurity run your life."
~Thema Davis

"Dream as if you'll live forever. Live as if you'll die today."

~James Dean

"The gratification comes in the doing, not in the results."
~James Dean

"For true success ask yourself these four questions: Why? Why not? Why not me? Why not now?"

~Jimmy Dean

"A woman knows the face of the man she loves as a sailor knows the open sea."

~Honore de Balzac

"A kiss is a rosy dot over the 'I' of loving."

~Cyrano de Bergerac

"Humor is by far the most significant activity of the human brain."

~Edward De Bono

"I will never put my name on a product that does not have the best that is in me."

~John Deere

"Jealousy springs more from love of self than from love of another."

~Francois de La Rochefoucauld

"There is no disguise which can hide love for long where it exists, or simulate it where it does not."

~Francois de La Rochefoucauld

"There are four questions of value in life... What is sacred?

Of what is the spirit made? What is worth living for, and what is worth dying for? The answer to each is the same. Only love."

~Johnny Depp

"A rock pile ceases to be a rock pile the moment a single man contemplates it, bearing within him the image of a cathedral."

~Antoine de Saint-Exupery

"Life has taught us that love does not consist in gazing at each other but in looking outward together in the same direction."

~Antoine de Saint-Exupery

"You just keep pushing. You just keep pushing. I made every mistake that could be made. But I just kept pushing."

~Rene Descartes

"If you try anything, if you try to lose weight, or to improve yourself, or to love, or to make the world a better place, you have already achieved something wonderful, before you even begin. Forget failure. If things don't work out the way you want, hold your head up high and be proud. And try again. And again. And again!"

~Sarah Dessen

"You should never be surprised when someone treats you with respect, you should expect it."

~Sarah Dessen

"There is nothing in the world so irresistibly contagious as laughter and good humor."
~Charles Dickens

"That it will never come again is what makes life so sweet."

~Emily Dickinson

"We turn not older with years but newer every day."

~Emily Dickinson

"Where thou are, that is home."

~Emily Dickinson

"Difficult times have helped me to understand better than before, how infinitely rich and beautiful life is in every way, and that so many things that one goes worrying about are of no importance whatsoever."

~Isak Dinesen

"All our dreams can come true – if we have the courage to pursue them."

~Walt Disney

"All the adversity I've had in my life, all my troubles and obstacles, have strengthened me... You may not realize it when it happens, but a kick in the teeth may be the best thing in the world for you."
~Walt Disney

"If you can dream it, you can do it."

~Walt Disney

"Our heritage and ideals, our code and standards -- the things we live by and teach our children -- are preserved or diminished by how freely we exchange ideas and feelings."

~Walt Disney

"The more you are like yourself, the less you are like anyone else, which makes you unique."

~Walt Disney

"There isn't a single human being who hasn't plenty to cry over, and the trick is to make the laughs outweigh the tears."

~Dorothy Dix

"Don't marry the person you think you can live with; marry the individual you think you can't live without."
~James C. Dobson

"When you're trying to motivate yourself, appreciate the fact that you're even thinking about making a change. And as you move forward, allow yourself to be good enough."

~Alice Domar

"In reality, the most important things happen when you don't look for them."

~Phil Donahue

"Love built on beauty, soon as beauty, dies."

~John Donne

"It's the little things you do that make the big things happen."

~Mike Dooley

"In order to love simply, it is necessary to know how to show love."

~Fyodor Dostoyevsky

"With love one can live even without happiness."
~Fyodor Dostoyevsky

"There is nothing more deceptive than an obvious fact."
~Arthur Conan Doyle

"Effective leadership is not about making speeches or being liked;
leadership is defined by results not attributes."
~Peter Drucker

"Management is doing things right; leadership is doing the right things."
~Peter Drucker

"Happiness is a state of mind and not a state of possession. Be as you are
and you will be happy, if you try to be someone else you will be miserable."
~Apoorve Dubey

"What is forgiven is usually well remembered."
~Louis Dudek

"Keeping ridiculous hours doesn't mean you'll be successful."
~Tony Dungy

"Be miserable. Or motivate yourself. Whatever has to be done, it's always
your choice."
~Wayne Dyer

"Patience can't be acquired overnight. It is just like building up a muscle. Every day you need to work on it."

~Eknath Easwaran

"The farther behind I leave the past, the closer I am to forging my own character."

~Isabelle Eberhardt

"I have friends in overalls whose friendship I would not swap for the favor of the kings of the world."

~Thomas Edison

"I have not failed. I've just found 10,000 ways that won't work."

~Thomas A. Edison

"Our greatest weakness lies in giving up. The most certain way to succeed is always to try just one more time."

~Thomas Edison

"The three great essentials to achieve anything worthwhile are: Hard work, Stick-to-itiveness, and Common sense."

~Thomas Edison

"There is no substitute for hard work."

~Thomas Edison

"Your worth consists in what you are and not in what you have."

~Thomas Edison

"A table, a chair, a bowl of fruit and a violin; what else does a man need to be happy?"

~Albert Einstein

"All religions, arts and sciences are branches of the same tree."

~Albert Einstein

"All that is valuable in human society depends upon the opportunity for development accorded the individual."

~Albert Einstein

"Any intelligent fool can make things bigger and more complex... It takes a touch of genius - and a lot of courage to move in the opposite direction."

~Albert Einstein

"Any man who can drive safely while kissing a pretty girl is simply not giving the kiss the attention it deserves."
~Albert Einstein

"Any man who reads too much and uses his own brain too little falls into lazy habits of thinking."

Albert Einstein

"Anyone who has never made a mistake has never tried anything new."
~Albert Einstein

"Anyone who doesn't take truth seriously in small matters cannot be trusted in large ones either."

~Albert Einstein

"Before God we are all equally wise - and equally foolish."

~Albert Einstein

"Common sense invents and constructs no less than its own field than science does in its domain. It is, however, in the nature of common sense not to be aware of this situation."

~Albert Einstein

"Common sense is the collection of prejudices acquired by age eighteen."

~Albert Einstein

"Education is what remains after one has forgotten what one has learned in school."

~Albert Einstein

"Everyone should be respected as an individual, but no one idolized."

~Albert Einstein

"Everything should be as simple as it is, but not simpler."

~Albert Einstein

"Everything that can be counted does not necessarily count; everything that counts cannot necessarily be counted."

~Albert Einstein

"Few are those who see with their own eyes and feel with their own hearts."

~Albert Einstein

"Few people are capable of expressing with equanimity opinions which differ from the prejudices of their social environment. Most people are even incapable of forming such opinions."

~Albert Einstein

"He who can no longer pause to wonder and stand rapt in awe, is as good as dead; his eyes are closed."

~Albert Einstein

"I have no special talents. I am only passionately curious."

~Albert Einstein

"I think and think for months and years. Ninety-nine times, the conclusion is false. The hundredth time I am right."

~Albert Einstein

"I used to go away for weeks in a state of confusion."
~Albert Einstein

"If you can't explain it simply, you don't understand it well enough."
~Albert Einstein

"If you want to live a happy life, tie it to a goal, not to people or things."
~Albert Einstein

"Imagination is everything. It is the preview of life's coming attractions."
~Albert Einstein

"Imagination is more important than knowledge."
~Albert Einstein

"In matters of truth and justice, there is no difference between large and small problems, for issues concerning the treatment of people are all the same."
~Albert Einstein

"In order to be an immaculate member of a flock of sheep, one must above all be a sheep oneself."
~Albert Einstein

"In the middle of difficulty lies opportunity."
~Albert Einstein

"Information is not knowledge."
~Albert Einstein

"Insanity: doing the same thing over and over again and expecting different results."
~Albert Einstein

"Intellectual growth should commence at birth and cease only at death."
~Albert Einstein

"Intellectuals solve problems, geniuses prevent them."
~Albert Einstein

"It is a miracle that curiosity survives formal education."
~Albert Einstein

"It's not that I'm so smart, it's just that I stay with problems longer."
~Albert Einstein

"Learn from yesterday, live for today, hope for tomorrow. The important thing is not to stop questioning."
~Albert Einstein

"Let every man be respected as an individual and no man idolized."
~Albert Einstein

"Life is like riding a bicycle. To keep your balance, you must keep moving."
~Albert Einstein

"Logic will get you from A to B. Imagination will take you everywhere."
~Albert Einstein

"Look deep into nature, and then you will understand everything better. "
~Albert Einstein

"Love is a better teacher than duty."
~Albert Einstein

"Many of the things you can count, don't count. Many of the things you can't count, really count."
~Albert Einstein

"Nothing happens until something moves."
~Albert Einstein

"Only a life lived for others is a life worthwhile."
~Albert Einstein

"Only one who devotes himself to a cause with his whole strength and soul can be a true master. For this reason mastery demands all of a person."
~Albert Einstein

"Peace cannot be kept by force; it can only be achieved by understanding."
~Albert Einstein

"People love chopping wood. In this activity one immediately sees results."
~Albert Einstein

"Solitude is painful when one is young, but delightful when one is more mature."
~Albert Einstein

"Strive not to be a success, but rather to be of value."
~Albert Einstein

"The difference between stupidity and genius is that genius has its limits."
~Albert Einstein

"The distinction between the past, present and future is only a stubbornly persistent illusion."
~Albert Einstein

"The hardest thing to understand in the world is the income tax."
~Albert Einstein

"The high destiny of the individual is to serve rather than to rule."
~Albert Einstein

"The important thing is not to stop questioning. Curiosity has its own reason for existing."
~Albert Einstein

"The pursuit of truth and beauty is a sphere of activity in which we are permitted to remain children all our lives."
~Albert Einstein

"You have to learn the rules of the game. And then you have to play better than anyone else."
~Albert Einstein

"Humility must always be the portion of any man who receives acclaim earned in the blood of his followers and the sacrifices of his friends."
~Dwight D. Eisenhower

"A problem is your chance to do your best."
~Duke Ellington

"Love is supreme and unconditional; like is nice but limited."
~Duke Ellington

"It is never too late to be what you might have been."
~George Elliot

"The strongest principle of growth lies in human choice."
~George Elliot

"Home is where one starts from."
~T.S. Eliot

"People to whom nothing has ever happened cannot understand the unimportance of events."

~T.S. Eliot

"There is no absolute point of view from which real and ideal can be finally separated and labeled."

~T.S. Eliot

"We shall not cease from exploration, and the end of all our exploring will be to arrive where we started and know the place for the first time."

~T.S. Eliot

"Perseverance is not a long race; it is many short races one after the other."
~Walter Elliot

"The best years of your life are the ones in which you decide your problems are your own. You do not blame them on your mother, the ecology, or the president. You realize that you control your own destiny."
~Albert Ellis

"Most people seek after what they do not possess and are thus enslaved by the very things they want to acquire."
~Anwar El-Sadat

A friend is one before whom I can think aloud."

~Ralph Waldo Emerson

"Adopt the pace of nature: her secret is patience."

~Ralph Waldo Emerson

"An ounce of action is worth a ton of theory."
~Ralph Waldo Emerson

"As a cure for worrying, work is better than whiskey."
~Ralph Waldo Emerson

"Character is higher than intellect. A great soul will be strong to live as well as think."

~Ralph Waldo Emerson

"Do not be too timid and squeamish about your actions. All life is an experiment. The more experiments you make the better. What if they are a little course, and you may get your coat soiled or torn? What if you do fail, and get fairly rolled in the dirt once or twice. Up again, you shall never be so afraid of a tumble."

~Ralph Waldo Emerson

"For every minute you are angry you lose sixty seconds of happiness."

~Ralph Waldo Emerson

"It is one of the blessings of old friends that you can afford to be stupid with them."

~Ralph Waldo Emerson

"The glory of friendship is not the outstretched hand, nor the kindly smile, nor the joy of companionship; it is the spiritual inspiration that comes to one when he discovers that someone else believes in him and is willing to trust him with friendship."
~Ralph Waldo Emerson

"We must be our own before we can be another's."

~Ralph Waldo Emerson

"Cherish your solitude. Take trains by yourself to places you have never been. Sleep out alone under the stars. Learn how to drive a stick shift. Go so far away that you stop being afraid of not coming back. Say no when you don't want to do something. Say yes if your instincts are strong, even if everyone around you disagrees. Decide whether you want to be liked or admired. Decide if fitting in is more important than finding out what you're doing here. Believe in kissing."

~Eve Ensler

"Difficulties are things that show a person what they are."

~Epictetus

"First say to yourself what you would be; and then do what you have to do."

~Epictetus

"If evil be spoken of you and it be true, correct yourself, if it be a lie, laugh at it."

~Epictetus

"If you do not wish to be prone to anger, do not feed the habit; give it nothing which may tend to its increase."

~Epictetus

"It is impossible to begin to learn that which one thinks one already knows."

~Epictetus

"It's not what happens to you, but how you react to it that matters."

~Epictetus

"No great thing is created suddenly."

~Epictetus

"One that desires to excel should endeavor in those things that are in themselves most excellent."

~Epitetus

"The greater the difficulty the more glory in surmounting it.

Skillful pilots gain their reputation from storms and tempests."

~Epictetus

"The key is to keep company only with people who uplift you, whose presence calls forth your best."

~Epitetus

"We cannot choose our external circumstances, but we can always choose how we respond to them."

~Epictetus

"We have two ears and one mouth so that we can listen twice as much as we speak."

~Epictetus

"Wealth consists not in having great possessions, but in having few wants."

~Epictetus

"Do not spoil what you have by desiring what you have not; but remember that what you now have was once among the things you only hoped for."

~Epicurus

"He is not a lover who does not love forever."

~Euripides

"The greatest pleasure of life is love."

~Euripides

"Tragedy, sadness, loneliness and despair taught me that life is really a beautiful thing; if it wasn't I wouldn't be able to recognize that anything was wrong"
~Greg Evans

"Children will not remember you for the material things you provided but for the feeling that you cherished them."

~Richard L. Evans

"Hard work spotlights the character of people: some turn up their sleeves, some turn up their noses, and some don't turn up at all."
~Sam Ewing

"A budget tells us what we can't afford, but it doesn't keep us from buying it."
~William Feather

"If we do not discipline ourselves the world will do it for us."
~William Feather

"No man is a failure who is enjoying life."

~William Feather

"The greatest results in life are usually attained by simple means and the exercise of ordinary qualities. These may for the most part be summed in these two: common-sense and perseverance."
~ Owen Feltham

"I don't have to attend every argument I'm invited to."

~W. C. Fields

"No one rises above who he or she has been without first having fallen down. The best time -- in fact, the only time -- to make a real change in your life is in the moment of seeing the need for it. He who hesitates always gets lost in the hundred reasons why tomorrow is a better day to get started."

~Guy Finley

"You get the best out of others when you get the best out of yourself."

~Harvey S. Firestone

"One of the many things nobody ever tells you about middle age is that it's such a nice change from being young."

~Dorothy Canfield Fisher

"It was only a sunny smile, and little it cost in the giving, but like morning light it scattered the night and made the day worth living."
~F. Scott Fitzgerald

"Our lives are defined by opportunities, even the ones we miss."
~F. Scott Fitzgerald

"The greatest act of courage is to be and to own all of who you are -- without apology, without excuses, without masks to cover the truth of who you are."
~Debbie Ford

"When you invoke the agent of change called acceptance, you must accept all that you are, all that you've been and all that you will be in the future."
~Debbie Ford

"An idealist is a person who helps other people to be prosperous."
~Henry Ford

"Anyone who stops learning is old, whether at twenty or eighty. Anyone who keeps learning stays young. The greatest thing in life is to keep your mind young."
~Henry Ford

"Don't find fault, find a remedy. "
~Henry Ford

"Failure is simply the opportunity to begin again, this time more intelligently."
~Henry Ford

"Obstacles are those frightful things you see when you take your eyes off your goal."
~Henry Ford

"There isn't a person anywhere who isn't capable of doing more than he thinks he can."
~Henry Ford

"All changes, even the most longed for, have their melancholy; for what we leave behind us is a part of ourselves; we must die to one life before we can enter another."
~Anatole France

"An education isn't how much you have committed to memory, or even how much you know. It's being able to differentiate between what you know and what you don't."
~Anatole France

"Lord, grant that I might not so much seek to be loved as to love."

~Francis of Assisi

"And finally I twist my heart round again, so that the bad is on the outside and the good is on the inside, and keep on trying to find a way of becoming what I would so like to be, and could be, if there weren't any other people living in the world."
~Anne Frank

"The last of the human freedoms is to choose one's attitude in any given set of circumstances."

~V. Frankl

"A house is not a home unless it contains food and fire for the mind as well as the body."
~Benjamin Franklin

"By failing to prepare, you are preparing to fail."
~Benjamin Franklin

"Remember not only to say the right thing in the right place, but far more difficult still, to leave unsaid the wrong thing at the tempting moment."
~Benjamin Franklin

"Speak little; do much. Well done is better than well said."
~Benjamin Franklin

"Trouble knocked at the door, but, hearing laughter, hurried away"
~Benjamin Franklin

"Your net worth to the world is usually determined by what remains after your bad habits are subtracted from your good ones."
~Benjamin Franklin

"There is no pillow so soft as a clear conscience."
~French Proverb

"I was always looking outside myself for strength and confidence, but it comes from within. It is there all the time."
~Anna Freud

"Aging is not lost youth but a new stage of opportunity and strength."
~Betty Friedan

"Love is the only sane and satisfactory answer to the problem of human existence."
~Erich Fromm

"A diplomat is a man who always remembers a woman's birthday but never remembers her age."
~Robert Frost

"A person will sometimes devote all his life to the development of one part of his body – the wishbone."

~Robert Frost

"Love is an irresistible desire to be irresistibly desired."

~Robert Frost

"Never be bullied into silence. Never allow yourself to be made a victim. Accept no one's definition of your life; define yourself."

~Robert Frost

"I believe that imagination is stronger than knowledge. That myth is more potent than history. That dreams are more powerful than facts. That hope always triumphs over experience. That laughter is the only cure for grief. And I believe that love is stronger than death."

~Robert Fulghum

"Choose a wife rather by your ear than your eye."

~Thomas Fuller

"He that cannot forgive others breaks the bridge over which he must pass himself; for every man has need to be forgiven."
~Thomas Fuller

"Love is a game that two can play and both win."
~Eva Gabor

"A man in love is incomplete until he has married – then he's finished."
~Zsa Zsa Gabor

"Don't you ever let a soul in the world tell you that you can't be exactly who you are."
~Lady Gaga

"It doesn't matter who you are, or where you come from, or how much money you've got in your pocket. You have your own destiny and your own life ahead of you."
~Lady Gaga

"Don't be too hard on yourself. There are plenty of people willing to do that for you. Love yourself and be proud of everything that you do. Even mistakes mean you're trying."
~Susan Gale

"Never forget where you've been. Never lose sight of where you're going. And never take for granted the people who travel the journey with you."
~Susan Gale

"Sometimes you don't realize your own strength until you come face to face with your greatest weakness."
~Susan Gale

"I refuse to lower my standards to accommodate people who refuse to raise theirs."
~Steve Gamlin

"People tend to forget their duties but remember their rights."
~Indira Gandhi

"There are two kinds of people, those who do the work and those who take the credit. Try to be in the first group; there is less competition there."
~Indira Gandhi

"You can't shake hands with a clenched fist."
~Indira Gandhi

"A small body of determined spirits fired by an unquenchable faith in their mission can alter the course of history."
~Mahatma Gandhi

"An eye for an eye only ends up making the whole world blind."
~Mahatma Gandhi

"Happiness is when what you think, what you say, and what you do are all in harmony."
~Mahatma Gandhi

"Live as if you were to die tomorrow. Learn as if you were to live forever."
~Mahatma Gandhi

"We must be the change we want to see."
~Mahatma Gandhi

"Where there is love there is life."
~Mahatma Gandhi

"Having more joy does not necessarily require a life overhaul -- you may just need to create more space in your life for moments of joy."

~Debrena Jackson Gandy

"I have had many troubles in my life, but the worst of them never came."

~James Garfield

"A boy is better unborn, than untaught."

~Caroline L. Gascoigne

"An error gracefully acknowledged is a victory won."

~Caroline L. Gascoigne

"The secret of health for both mind and body is not to mourn for the past, nor to worry about the future, but to live the present moment wisely and earnestly."

~Siddhartha Gautama

"To love is to admire with the heart; to admire is to love with the mind."

~Theophile Gautier

"It is well to give when asked but it is better to give unasked, through understanding."

~Kahlil Gibran

"Love is trembling happiness."

~Khalil Gibran

"Your living is determined not so much by what life brings to you as by the attitude you bring to life; not so much by what happens to you as by the way your mind looks at what happens."

~Khalil Gibran

Follow Your Dreams

"You need to learn how to select your thoughts just the same way you select your clothes every day. This is a power you can cultivate. If you want to control things in your life so bad, work on the mind. That's the only thing you should be trying to control."

~Elizabeth Gilbert

"Follow your inner moonlight; don't hide the madness."

~Allen Ginsberg

"People will try to rain on your parade because they have no parade of their own."

~Jeffrey Gitomer

"A true friend never gets in your way unless you happen to be going down."
~Arnold H. Glasow

"Nothing last forever – not even your troubles."

~Arnold Glasgow

"Treat people as if they were what they ought to be and you help them become what they are capable of becoming."

~Goethe

"Whatever you can do, or dream you can do, begin it. Boldness has genius, power and magic in it."

~Goethe

"A mind too vigorous and active, serves only to consume the body to which it is joined."

~Oliver Goldsmith

"The harder I work, the luckier I get."

~Samuel Goldwyn

"What you do makes a difference, and you have to decide what kind of difference you want to make."

~Jane Goodall

"We spend January 1 walking through our lives, room by room, drawing up a list of work to be done, cracks to be patched. Maybe this year, to balance the list, we ought to walk through the rooms of our lives... not looking for flaws, but for potential."

~Ellen Goodman

"A man has cause for regret only when he sows and no one reaps."
~Charles Goodyear

"When one loves somebody, everything is clear – where to go, what to do – it all takes care of itself and on doesn't have to ask anybody about anything."

~Maxim Gorky

"Attempt easy tasks as if they were difficult, and difficult as if they were easy; in the one case that confidence may not fall asleep, in the other that it may not be dismayed."

~Baltasar Gracian

"Is much to gain universal admiration; more universal love."

~Baltasar Gracian

"To love what you do and feel that it matters -- how could anything be more fun?"

~Katharine Graham

"Shared laughter creates a bond of friendships. When people laugh together, they cease to be young and old, teacher and pupils, worker and boss. They become a single group of human beings."

~W. Lee Grant

"The successful person has the habit of doing the things failures don't like to do. They don't like doing them either necessarily. But their disliking is subordinated to the strength of their purpose."

~E.M Gray

"You need to know what life you want (as well as what life you don't want), then you have to muster up the will and the drive to go after it."
~Bob Greene

"A heart that loves is always young."

~Greek Proverb

"You'll always miss 100% of the shots you don't take."

~Wayne Gretzky

"We could have bought a small yacht with what we spent on our dog and all the things he destroyed. Then again, how many yachts wait by the door all day for your return?"

~John Grogan

"You can pretend to be serious; you can't pretend to be witty."

~Sacha Guitry

"Life has got a habit of not standing hitched. You got to ride it like you find it. You got to change with it. If a day goes by that don't change some of your old notions for new ones, that is just about like trying to milk a dead cow."

~Woody Guthrie

"This art of resting the mind and the power of dismissing from it all care and worry is probably one of the secrets of energy in our great men."
~Captain J. A. Hadfield

"Even after all this time, the sun never says to the earth 'you owe me.' Just think what a love like that can do? It lights up the whole world."
~Hafiz

"Never bear more than one trouble at a time. Some people bear three kinds -- all they have had, all they have now, and all they expect to have."
~Edward Everett Hale

"Nobody can do for little children what grandparents do.
Grandparents sort of sprinkle stardust over the lives of little children."
~Alex Haley

"Belief is passive. Faith is active."
~Edith Hamilton

"Forgiveness is the answer to the child's dream of a miracle by which what is broken is made whole again, what is soiled is made clean again."
~Dag Hammarskjold

"The early bird gets the worm, but the second mouse gets the cheese."
~Jon Hammond

"If we believe that tomorrow will be better, we can bear a hardship today."
~Thich Nhat Hanh

"Smile, breathe and go slowly."

~Thich Nhat Hanh

"Eating everything you want is not that much fun. When you live a life with no boundaries, there's less joy. If you can eat anything you want to, what's the fun in eating anything you want to?"

~Tom Hanks

"Don't be afraid your life will end. Be afraid that it will never begin."

~Grace Hansen

"A daily routine built on good habits and disciplines separates the most successful among us from everyone else. The routine is exceptionally powerful."

~Darren Hardy

"You have to take your shots when you get them. I learned that the one thing that never comes back is a missed opportunity."

~Devon Harris

"Never take the advice of someone who has not had your kind of trouble."

~Sidney J. Harris

"I've come to believe that seeking happiness is not a frivolous pursuit. It's honorable and necessary. And most people forget even to think about it."

~Goldie Hawn

"Happiness is like a butterfly which, when pursued, is always beyond our grasp, but, if you will sit down quietly, may alight upon you."

~Nathaniel Hawthorne

"People often say that 'beauty is in the eye of the beholder,' and I say that the most liberating thing about beauty is realizing that you are the beholder. This empowers us to find beauty in places where others have not dared to look, including inside ourselves."

~Salma Hayek

"If you think you can win, you can win. Faith is necessary to victory."

~William Hazlitt

"When in doubt, make a fool of yourself. There's a thin line between being brilliantly creative and acting like the biggest idiot on earth."

~Cynthia Heimel

"Things start out as hopes and end up as habits."

~Lillian Hellman

"About morals, I know only that what is moral is what you feel good after and what is immoral is what you feel bad after."

~Ernest Hemingway

"Always do sober what you said you'd do drunk. That will teach you to keep your mouth shut."

~Ernest Hemingway

"Every man's life ends the same way. It is only the details of how he lived and how he died that distinguish one man from another."

~Ernest Hemingway

"The world breaks everyone, and afterward, some are strong at the broken places."

~Ernest Hemingway

"When the power of love overcomes the love of power, the world will finally know Peace."

~Jimi Hendrix

Follow Your Dreams

"After a storm comes a calm."
Matthew Henry

"I believe in pink. I believe that laughing is the best calorie burner. I believe in kissing, kissing a lot. I believe in being strong when everything seems to be going wrong. I believe that happy girls are the prettiest girls. I believe that tomorrow is another day and I believe in miracles."

~Audrey Hepburn

"I love people who make me laugh. I honestly think it's the thing I like most, to laugh. It cures a multitude of ills.

It's probably the most important thing in a person."

~Audrey Hepburn

"Nothing is impossible; the word itself says I'm possible!"

~Audrey Hepburn

"Remember, if you ever need a helping hand, you'll find one at the end of your arm. As you grow older you will discover that you have two hands. One for helping yourself, the other for helping others."

~Audrey Hepburn

"If you always do what interests you, at least one person is pleased."

~Katharine Hepburn

"Big results require big ambitions."

~Heraclitus

"The way up and the way down are one and the same."

~Heraclitus

"Be yourself. No one can ever tell you you're doing it wrong."

~James Leo Herlihy

"Wonder rather than doubt is the root of all knowledge."

~Abraham Joshua Heschel

"Before success comes in any man's life, he's sure to meet with much temporary defeat and, perhaps some failures. When defeat overtakes a man, the easiest and the most logical thing to do is to quit. That's exactly what the majority of men do."
~Napoleon Hill

"Every problem or difficulty you face contains the seed of an equal or greater advantage or benefit."

~Napoleon Hill

"Great achievement is usually born of great sacrifice, and is never the result of selfishness."

~Napoleon Hill

"It is not the mountain we conquer but ourselves."
~ Edmund Hillary

"The willingness to forgive is a sign of spiritual and emotional maturity. It is one of the great virtues to which we all should aspire. Imagine a world filled with individuals willing both to apologize and to accept an apology. Is there any problem that could not be solved among people who possessed the humility and largeness of spirit and soul to do either -- or both -- when needed?"

~Gordon B. Hinckley

"Without hard work, nothing grows but weeds."

~Gordon B. Hinckley

"There are hundreds of paths up the mountain, all leading to the same place, so it doesn't matter which path you take. The only person wasting time is the one who runs around the mountain, telling everyone that his or her path is wrong."

~Hindu proverb

"Make a habit of two things: to help; or at least to do no harm."

~Hippocrates

"As you walk down the fairway of life you must smell the roses, for you only get to play one round."
~Ben Hogan

"Compassion is the antitoxin of the soul: where there is compassion even the most poisonous impulses remain relatively harmless."

~Eric Hoffer

"Love is like a faucet, it turns off and on."

~Billie Holiday

"Look at your past. Your past has determined where you are at this moment. What you do today will determine where you are tomorrow. Are you moving forward or standing still?"

~Tom Hopkins

"Cease to inquire what the future has in store, and take as a gift whatever the day brings forth."

~Horace

"Life is largely a matter of expectation."

~Horace

"Fortunately analysis is not the only way to resolve inner conflicts. Life itself still remains a very effective therapist."

~Karen Horney

"We all have the extraordinary coded within us, waiting to be released."

~Jean Houston

"Always walk through life as if you have something new to learn and you will."

~Vernon Howard

"Life in abundance comes only through great love."

~Elbert Hubbard

"The greatest mistake you can make in life is to continually be afraid you will make one."
~Elbert Hubbard

"Perfection is a road, not a destination. Every time I live, I get an education."

~Burk Hudson

"We are not on this earth to accumulate victories, things, and experiences, but to be whittled and sandpapered until what's left is who we truly are."

~Arianna Huffington

"An artist must be free to choose what he does, certainly, but he must also never be afraid to do what he might choose."

~Langston Hughes

"Emergencies have always been necessary to progress. It was darkness which produced the lamp. It was fog that produced the compass. It was hunger that drove us to exploration. And it took a depression to teach us the real value of a job."

~Victor Hugo

"Life is the flower for which love is the honey."

~Victor Hugo

Follow Your Dreams

"The supreme happiness of life is the conviction that we are loved."
~Victor Hugo

"A thing is might big when time and distance cannot shrink it."
~Zora Neale Hurston

"I love myself when I am laughing."
~Zora Neale Hurston

"There are years that ask questions and years that answer."
~Zora Neale Hurston

"There is no agony like bearing an untold story inside you."
~Zora Neale Hurston

"Dream in a pragmatic way."
~Aldous Huxley

"Maybe this world is another planet's Hell."
~Aldous Huxley

"The discipline of writing something down is the first step toward making it happen."
~Lee Iococca

"As you slide down the banister of life, may the splinters never point in the wrong direction."
~Irish blessing

"May you have the hindsight to know where you've been, the foresight to know where you're going, and the insight to know when you're going too far."
~Irish Blessing

"Trust me, but look to thyself."
~Irish Proverb

"I believe that education is all about being excited about something. Seeing passion and enthusiasm helps push an educational message."
~Steve Irwin

"Of all our possessions, wisdom alone is immortal."
~Isocrates

"If my mind can conceive it, and my heart can believe it, I know I can achieve it."
~Jesse Jackson

"You're blessed if you have strength to work."

~Mahalia Jackson

"If you enter this world knowing you are loved and you leave this world knowing the same, then everything that happens in between can be dealt with."

~Michael Jackson

"It's all right letting yourself go as long as you can let yourself back."

~Mick Jagger

"Act as if what you do makes a difference. It does."
~William James

"Nothing is so fatiguing as the eternal hanging on of an uncompleted task."

~William James

"Whenever you're in conflict with someone, there is one factor that can make the difference between damaging your relationship and deepening it. That factor is attitude."

~William James

"At least three times every day take a moment and ask yourself what is really important. Have the wisdom and the courage to build your life around your answer."

~Lee Jampolsky

"Forgiveness mean letting go of the past."

~Gerald Jampolsky

"A coward is much more exposed to quarrels than a man of spirit."
~Thomas Jefferson

"Determine never to be idle. No person will have occasion to complain of the want of time who never loses any. It is wonderful how much may be done if we are always doing."

~Thomas Jefferson

"Do you want to know who you are? Don't ask. Act! Action will delineate and define you."
~Thomas Jefferson

"In matters of style, swim with the current; in matters of principle, stand like a rock."

~Thomas Jefferson

"When you reach the end of your rope, tie a knot in it and hang on."
~Thomas Jefferson

"To err is human, but when the eraser wears out ahead of the pencil, you're overdoing it."

~Josh Jenkins

"Be a yardstick of quality. Some people aren't used to an environment where excellence is expected."

~Steve Jobs

"Being the richest man in the cemetery doesn't matter to me.
Going to bed at night saying we've done something wonderful...
that's what matters to me."
~Steve Jobs

"Don't let the noise of others opinions drown out your inner voice."
~Steve Jobs

"I didn't see it then, but it turned out that getting fired from Apple was the best thing that could have ever happened to me. The heaviness of being successful was replaced by the lightness of being a beginner again, less sure about everything. It freed me to enter one of the most creative periods of my life."
~Steve Jobs

"If you haven't found it yet, keep looking. Don't settle. As with all matters of the heart, you'll know when you find it.
And, like any great relationship, it just gets better and better as the years roll on."
~Steve Jobs

"Quality is more important than quantity. One home run is much better than two doubles."
~Steve Jobs

"Remembering that I'll be dead soon is the most important tool I've ever encountered to help me make the big choices in life. Because almost everything – all external expectations, all pride, all fear of embarrassment or failure – these things just fall away in the face of death, leaving only what is truly important. Remembering that you are going to die is the best way I know to avoid the trap of thinking you have something to lose. You are already naked. There is no reason not to follow your heart."
~Steve Jobs

"The only way to do great work is to love what you do. If you haven't found it yet, keep looking. Don't settle. As with all matters of the heart, you'll know when you find it."

~Steve Jobs

"You can't connect the dots looking forward; you can only connect them looking backwards. So you have to trust that the dots will somehow connect in your future. You have to trust in something — your gut, destiny, life, karma, whatever. This approach has never let me down, and it has made all the difference in my life."

~Steve Jobs

"Your work is going to fill a large part of your life, and the only way to be truly satisfied is to do what you believe is great work. And the only way to do great work is to love what you do. If you haven't found it yet, keep looking. Don't settle. As with all matters of the heart, you'll know when you find it. And, like any great relationship, it just gets better and better as the years roll on. So keep looking until you find it. Don't settle."

~Steve Jobs

"Love is the foundation from which your decisions about your life should be made."

~Darren L. Johnson

"I have learned that only two things are necessary to keep one's wife happy. First, let her think she's having her own way. And second, let her have it."

~Lyndon B. Johnson

"Things don't go wrong and break your heart so you can become bitter and give up. They happen to break you down and build you up so you can be all that you were intended to be."

~Samuel Johnson

"We come to love not by finding the perfect person, but by learning to see an imperfect person perfectly."

~Angelina Jolie

"Love and fear. Everything the father of a family says must inspire one or the other."

~Joseph Joubert

"To teach is to learn twice."

~Joseph Joubert

"When you go in search of honey you must expect to be stung by bees."

~Joseph Joubert

"A man's errors are his portals of discovery."

~James Joyce

"It is better to look ahead and prepare than to look back and regret."

~Jackie Joyner-Kersee

"The meeting of two personalities is like the contact of two chemical substances: if there is any reaction, both are transformed."
— C.G. Jung

"You must never feel badly about making mistakes as long as you take the trouble to learn from them. For you often learn more by being wrong for the right reasons than you do by being right for the wrong reasons."

~Norton Juster

"The things you do for yourself are gone when you are gone, but the things you do for others remain as your legacy."
~Kalu Kalu

"Never be satisfied with what you achieve, because it all pales in comparison with what you are capable of doing in the future."
~Rabbi Nochem Kaplan

"I think if I've learned anything about friendship, it's to hang in, stay connected, fight for them, and let them fight for you. Don't walk away, don't be distracted, don't be too busy or tired, don't take them for granted. Friends are part of the glue that holds life and faith together. Powerful stuff."

~Jon Katz

"A hug is like a boomerang -- you get it back right away."
~Bil Keane

"Alone we can do so little; together we can do so much."
~Helen Keller

"Although the world is full of suffering, it is also full of the overcoming of it."
~Helen Keller

"Face your deficiencies and acknowledge them; but do not let them master you. Let them teach you patience, sweetness, insight. When we do the best we can, we never know what miracle is wrought in our life, or in the life of another."

~Helen Keller

"Faith is knowing there is an ocean because there is a brook."

~Helen Keller

"Knowledge is love and light and vision."

~Helen Keller

"Life is either a daring adventure or nothing."

~Helen Keller

"Long term success is built on credibility and on establishing enduring loving relationships with quality people based on mutually earned trust. Cut all ties with dishonest, negative or lazy people, and associate with people who share your values. You become who you associate with."

~Dave Kekich

"Strive to increase order and discipline in your life.

Discipline usually means doing the opposite of what you feel like doing. The easy roads to discipline are setting deadlines; discovering and doing what you do best and what's important and enjoyable to you; focusing on habits by replacing your bad habits and thought patterns, one-by-one, over time, with good habits and thought patterns."

~Dave Kekich

"If you can learn from hard knocks, you can also learn from soft touches."

~Carolyn Kenmore

"Physical fitness is not only one of the most important keys to a healthy body, it is the basis of dynamic and creative intellectual activity."

~John F. Kennedy

"Each time someone stands up for an ideal, or acts to improve the lot of others, or strikes out against injustice, he sends forth a tiny ripple of hope."
~Robert F. Kennedy

"Great things are not accomplished by those who yield to trends and fads and popular opinion."

~Jack Kerouac

"People think love is an emotion. Love is good sense."

~Ken Kesey

"No one would have crossed the ocean if he could have gotten off the ship in the storm."

~Charles Kettering

"Even if you fall on your face, you're still moving forward."
Victor Kiam

"Every little thing wants to be loved."

~Sue Monk Kidd

"People demand freedom of speech to make up for the freedom of thought which they avoid."

~Soren Aabye Kierkegaard

"Smart people know their strengths, but happy people are the ones who have accepted their flaws."
~ Kimo

"At the center of non-violence stands the principle of love."

~Martin Luther King, Jr.

"Darkness cannot drive out darkness; only light can do that.

Hate cannot drive out hate; only love can do that."

~Martin Luther King, Jr.

"Discrimination is a hellhound that gnaws at Negroes in every waking moment of their lives to remind them that the lie of their inferiority is accepted as truth in the society dominating them."

~Martin Luther King, Jr.

"Faith is taking the first step even when you can't see the whole staircase."

~Martin Luther King, Jr.

"I may be crucified for my beliefs and, if I am, you can say, "He died to make men free."

~Martin Luther King, Jr.

"If a man hasn't discovered something that he would die for, he isn't fit to live."

~Martin Luther King, Jr.

"If a man is called to be a street sweeper, he should sweep streets even as Michelangelo painted, or Beethoven composed music or Shakespeare wrote poetry. He should sweep streets so well that all the hosts of heaven and earth will pause to say, 'Here lived a great street sweeper who did his job well."

~Martin Luther King Jr.

"In the End, we will remember not the words of our enemies, but the silence of our friends."

~Martin Luther King Jr.

"Nothing in all the world is more dangerous than sincere ignorance and conscientious stupidity."

~Martin Luther King, Jr.

"The time is always right to do what is right."

~Martin Luther King, Jr.

"The ultimate measure of a man is not where he stands in moments of comfort, but where he stands at times of challenge and controversy."
~Martin Luther King, Jr.

"The place where you made your stand never mattered. Only that you were there... and still on your feet."

~Stephen King

"Don't try to figure out what other people want to hear from you; figure out what you have to say. It's the one and only thing you have to offer."

~Barbara Kingsolver

"The very least you can do in your life is figure out what you hope for. And the most you can do is live inside that hope.

Not admire it from a distance but live right in it, under its roof."

~Barbara Kingsolver

"If I've learned one lesson from all that's happened to me, it's that there is no such thing as the biggest mistake of your existence. There's no such thing as ruining your life.

Life's a pretty resilient thing, it turns out."

~Sophie Kinsella

"Accept everything about yourself - I mean everything, You are you and that is the beginning and the end - no apologies, no regrets."
~Henry A. Kissinger

"A rose is not its thorns, a peach is not its fuzz and a human being is not his or her crankiness."

~Lisa Kogan

"I really believe that everyone has a talent, ability, or skill that he can mine to support himself and to succeed in life."

~Dean Koontz

Follow Your Dreams

"The knowledge of the past stays with us. To let go is to release the images and emotions, the grudges and fears, the clingings and disappointments of the past that bind our spirit."

~Jack Kornfield

"Pick battles big enough to matter, small enough to win."

~Jonathan Kozol

"Experiences are savings which a miser puts aside. Wisdom is an inheritance which a wastrel cannot exhaust."
~Karl Kraus

"If you only do what you know you can do- you never do very much."
~Tom Krause

"If an egg is broken by outside force, Life ends. If broken by inside force, Life begins. Great things always begin from inside."

~Jim Kwik

"The only real prison is fear, and the only real freedom is freedom from fear."

~Aung San Suu Kyi

"Be kind whenever possible. It is always possible."
~Dalai Lama

"Happiness is not something ready made. It comes from your own actions."
~Dalai Lama

"It is necessary to help others, not only in our prayers, but in our daily lives. If we find we cannot help others, the least we can do is to desist from harming them."
~Dalai Lama

"Our prime purpose in this life is to help others. And if you can't help them, at least don't hurt them."
~Dalai Lama

"You have to make mistakes to find out who you aren't. You take the action, and the insight follows: You don't think your way into becoming yourself."
~Anne Lamott

"Nobody gets to live life backward. Look ahead, that is where you future lies."
~Ann Landers

"Some people believe holding on and hanging in there are signs of great strength. However, there are times when it takes much more strength to know when to let go and then do it."
~Ann Landers

Follow Your Dreams

"A clever man reaps some benefit from the worst catastrophe, and a fool can turn even good luck to his disadvantage."

~Francois de La Rochefoucauld

"The difference between the possible and the impossible lies in a person's determination."
~Tommy Lasorda

"Pressure is a word that is misused in our vocabulary. When you start thinking of pressure, it's because you've started to think of failure."
~Tommy Lasorda

"Decision and determination are the engineer and fireman of our train to opportunity and success."

~Burt Lawlor

"All men dream, but not equally. Those who dream by night in the dusty recesses of their minds, wake in the day to find that it was vanity: but the dreamers of the day are dangerous men, for they may act on their dreams with open eyes, to make them possible."
~T. E. Lawrence

"A goal is not always meant to be reached, it often serves simply as something to aim at."
~Bruce Lee

"I fear not the man who has practiced 10,000 kicks once, but I fear the man who has practiced one kick 10,000 times."
~ Bruce Lee

"If you love life, don't waste time, for time is what life is made up of."
~Bruce Lee

"Mistakes are always forgivable, if one has the courage to admit them."
~Bruce Lee

"Nature is forever arriving and forever departing, forever approaching, forever vanishing; but in her vanishings there seems to be ever the waving of a hand, in all her partings a promise of meetings farther along the road."

~Richard Le Gallienne

"People do not always make breakthroughs because they refused to quit. Sometimes they make them because they know when to quit. When they realize that enough is enough, that old patterns aren't serving them, that it's time to repack their bags."

~Richard J. Leider

"Work like you don't need the money, love like you've never been hurt and dance like no one is watching."

~Randall G. Leighton

"I bet there are things you are holding onto that simply are no longer worthy of your time. It's not that they're not worthy goals for someone... they're just not goals worthy of your life. But it's just not a good use of your life to hang on. Think big, act big. Don't be afraid to move on."

~Jason Leister

"Count your age by friends, not years. Count your life by smiles, not tears."

~John Lennon

"There are two basic motivating forces: fear and love. When we are afraid, we pull back from life. When we are in love, we open to all that life has to offer with passion, excitement, and acceptance. We need to learn to love ourselves first, in all our glory and our imperfections. If we cannot love ourselves, we cannot fully open to our ability to love others or our potential to create. Evolution and all hopes for a better world rest in the fearlessness and open-hearted vision of people who embrace life."

~John Lennon

"Love the flower you've got to let grow."

~John Lennon

Follow Your Dreams

"You don't need anybody to tell you who you are or what you are. You are what you are!"

~John Lennon

"You may say I'm a dreamer, but I'm not the only one. I hope someday you'll join us. And the world will live as one."

~John Lennon

"We need to learn to love ourselves first, in all our glory and our imperfections. If we cannot love ourselves, we cannot fully open to our ability to love others or our potential to create. Evolution and all hopes for a better world rest in the fearlessness and open-hearted vision of people who embrace life."

~John Lennon

"The game of life is not so much in holding a good hand as playing a poor hand well."

~H. T. Leslie

"Agree to these ground rules: Be curious, conversational and real. Don't persuade or interrupt. Listen, listen, listen."

~Elizabeth Lesser

"There is only one real sin, and that is to persuade oneself that the second-best is anything but the second-best."
~Doris Lessing

"Remember that at any given moment there are a thousand things you can love."

~David Levithan

"The things you hope for the most are the things that destroy you in the end."

~David Levithan

"Courage is not simply one of the virtues, but the form of every virtue at the testing point."
~C.S. Lewis

"Getting over a painful experience is much like crossing monkey bars. You have to let go at some point in order to move forward."
~C.S. Lewis

"You are never too old to set another goal or to dream a new dream."
~C.S. Lewis

"One's first step in wisdom is to question everything - and one's last is to come to terms with everything."
- Georg C. Lichtenberg

"Always bear in mind that your own resolution to succeed is more important than any other."
~Abraham Lincoln

"And in the end, it's not the years in your life that count. It's the life in your years."
~Abraham Lincoln

"Be sure to put your feet in the right place, and then stand firm."
~Abraham Lincoln

"I do not think much of a man who is not wiser today than he was yesterday."
~Abraham Lincoln

"Important principles may, and must, be inflexible."
~Abraham Lincoln

Follow Your Dreams

"Rules of living: Don't worry, eat three square meals a day, say your prayers, be courteous to your creditors, keep your digestion good, steer clear of biliousness, exercise, go slow and go easy. Maybe there are other things that your special case requires to make you happy, but, my friend, these, I reckon, will give you a good life."

~Abraham Lincoln

"Tact is the ability to describe others as they see themselves."

~Abraham Lincoln

"The best way to destroy an enemy is to make him a friend."

~Abraham Lincoln

"Whatever you are, be a good one."
~Abraham Lincoln

"You can have anything you want, if you want it badly enough. You can be anything you want to be, do anything you set out to accomplish if you hold to that desire with singleness of purpose."
~Abraham Lincoln

"Life is like a landscape. You live in the midst of it but can describe it only from the vantage point of distance."

~Charles Lindbergh

"Dictionary is the only place that success comes before work. Hard work is the price we must pay for success. I think you can accomplish anything if you're willing to pay the price."
~Vince Lombardi

"It's easy to have faith in yourself and have discipline when you're a winner, when you're number one. What you got to have is faith and discipline when you're not a winner."
~Vince Lombardi

"People who work together will win, whether it be against complex football defenses, or the problems of modern society."
~ Vince Lombardi

"The difference between a successful person and others is not a lack of strength, not a lack of knowledge, but rather a lack of will."
~Vince Lombardi

"The measure of who we are is what we do with what we have."
~Vince Lombardi

"The price of success is hard work, dedication to the job at hand, and the determination that whether we win or lose, we have applied the best of ourselves to the task at hand."
~Vince Lombardi

"Winning isn't everything, but wanting to win is."

~Vince Lombardi

"You can't wait for inspiration, you have to go after it with club."

~Jack London

"Here is the test to find whether your mission on Earth is finished: if you're alive, it isn't."
~Alice Roosevelt Longworth

"I have a simple philosophy: Fill what's empty. Empty what's full. Scratch where it itch

~Alice Roosevelt Longworth

"That love for one, from which there doth not spring wide love for all, is but a worthless thing."

~James Russell Lowell

"To lead the orchestra, you have to turn your back on the crowd."

~Max Lucado

Follow Your Dreams

"You change your life by changing your heart."
~Max Lucado

"Holding on to anger, resentment and hurt only gives you tense muscles, a headache and a sore jaw from clenching your teeth.

Forgiveness gives you back the laughter and the lightness in your life."

~Joan Lunden

"It is better to be feared than loved, if you cannot be both."
~Niccolo Machiavelli

"There is nothing more difficult to take in hand, more perilous to conduct, or more uncertain of its success than to take the lead of a new order of things."
~Niccolo Machiavelli

"I used to think that anyone doing anything weird was weird. I suddenly realized that anyone doing anything weird wasn't weird at all and it was the people saying they were weird that were weird."
~Paul McCartney

"To be trusted is a greater compliment than being loved."
~George MacDonald

"True love is quiescent, except in the nascent moments of true humility."
~Bryant H. McGill

"Life is too short to wake up with regrets. So love the people who treat you right. Forget about those who don't. Believe everything happens for a reason. If you get a chance, take it. If it changes your life, let it. Nobody said life would be easy, they just promised it would most likely be worth it."
~Harvey MacKay

"Love is the silent saying and saying of a single name."
~Mignon McLaughlin

"A man who trusts nobody is apt to be the kind of man nobody trusts."
~Harold MacMillan

"And as we let our own light shine, we unconsciously give other people permission to do the same."
~Nelson Mandela

"I learned that courage was not the absence of fear, but the triumph over it. The brave man is not he who does not feel afraid, but he who conquers that fear."
~Nelson Mandela

"If you want to make peace with your enemy, you have to work with your enemy. Then he becomes your partner."
~Nelson Mandela

"It always seems impossible until it's done."
~Nelson Mandela

"Always do your best. What you plant now, you will harvest later."
Og Mandino

"The mindless junk of your past crowds out opportunities and sets pointless limitations. Move out the junk, and you create room for the rest of your life. Ultimately, it's not just a question of tidying your house; it's a question of liberating your heart."
~Merlin Mann

"If you have a goal, write it down. If you do not write it down, you do not have a goal -- you have a wish."
~Steve Maraboli

"Incredible change happens in your life when you decide to take control of what you do have power over instead of craving control over what you don't."
~Steve Maraboli

"It only takes a split second to smile and forget, yet to someone that needed it, it can last a lifetime."

~Steve Maraboli

"Make a pact with yourself today to not be defined by your past. Sometimes the greatest thing to come out of all your hard work isn't what you get for it, but what you become for it. Shake things up today! Be You... Be Free... Share."

~Steve Maraboli

"Renew, release, let go. Yesterday's gone. There's nothing you can do to bring it back. You can't 'should've' done something. You can only DO something. Renew yourself. Release that attachment. Today is a new day!"

~Steve Maraboli

"Love never fails. Character never quits. And with patience and persistence, dreams do come true."

~ Pete Maravich

"Successful leaders see the opportunities in every difficulty rather than the difficulty in every opportunity."

~Reed Markham

"There is no medicine like hope, no incentive so great and no tonic so powerful as expectation of something tomorrow."

~O.S. Marden

"When a thing is done, it's done. Don't look back. Look forward to your next objective."

~George C. Marshall

"Rest when you're weary. Refresh and renew yourself, your body, your mind, your spirit. Then get back to work."

~Ralph Marston

"What you do today can improve all your tomorrows."

~Ralph Marston

"Each morning when I open my eyes I say to myself: I, not events, have the power to make me happy or unhappy today. I can choose which it shall be. Yesterday is dead, tomorrow hasn't arrived yet. I have just one day, today, and I'm going to be happy in it.
~Groucho Marx

"I, not events, have the power to make me happy or unhappy today. I can choose which it shall be. Yesterday is dead, tomorrow hasn't arrived yet. I have just one day, today, and I'm going to be happy in it."

~Groucho Marx

"She's a lovely person. She deserves a good husband. Marry her before she finds one."

~Harpo Marx

"Anyone who knows anything of history knows that great social changes are impossible without feminine upheaval. Social progress can be measured exactly by the social position of the fair sex, the ugly ones included."

~Karl Marx

"One can choose to go back toward safety or forward toward growth. Growth must be chosen again and again; fear must be overcome again and again."

~Abraham Maslow

"Go after your dream, no matter how unattainable others think it is."

~Linda Mastandrea

"Before you can learn a new way of doing things, you have to unlearn the old way. So beginnings depend on endings."

~Rick Maurer

"Life is 10% of what happens to me and 90% of how I react to it."

~John Maxwell

"Stay away from fire fighters because they will douse your flames....stick close with fire lighters because they will always help you keep the flame burning under your dreams and goals."

~John Maxwell

"You will never change your life until you change something you do daily. The secret of your success is found in your daily routine."

~John Maxwell

"If you had started doing anything two weeks ago, by today you would have been two weeks better at it."

~John Mayer

"Happiness is like a kiss. You must share it to enjoy it."

~Bernard Meltzer

"It's better to fail in originality, than succeed in imitation."

~Herman Melville

"Unrest of spirit is a mark of life; one problem after another presents itself and in the solving of them we can find our greatest pleasure."
~Kal Menninger

"Wise people listen more than they talk."

~Joyce Meyer

"Trust that little voice in your head that says 'Wouldn't it be interesting if...' And then do it."

~Duane Michals

"I saw the angel in the marble and carved until I set him free."
~Michelangelo

"Lord, grant that I may always desire more than I can accomplish."

~Michelangelo

"The greatest danger for most of us is not that our aim is too high and we miss it but that it is too low and we reach it."

~Michelangelo

"To the world you might be one person, but to one person you might be the world."

~Ebony Mikle

"When you stop expecting people to be perfect, you can like them for who they are."
~Donald Miller

"Life moves on, whether we act as cowards or heroes.

Everything we shut our eyes to, everything we run away from, everything we deny, denigrate, or despise, serves to defeat us in the end. What seems nasty, painful, or evil can become a source of beauty, joy and strength, if faced with an open mind. Every moment is a golden one for him who has the vision to recognize it as such."

~Henry Miller

"If you will call your troubles experiences, and remember that every experience develops some latent force within you, you will grow vigorous and happy, however adverse your circumstances may seem to be."

~John R. Miller

"Weeds are flowers, too, once you get to know them."

~A.A. Milne

"Be nice to people on your way up because you'll meet them on your way down."
~Wilson Mizner

"The best way to keep your friends is not to give them away."
~Wilson Mizner

"The best day of your life is the one on which you decide your life is your own. No apologies or excuses. No one to lean on, rely on, or blame. The gift is yours -- it is an amazing journey -- and you alone are responsible for the quality of it. This is the day your life really begins."
~Bob Moawad

"Everyone's a star and deserves the right to twinkle."
~Marilyn Monroe

"I believe that everything happens for a reason. People change so that you can learn to let go, things go wrong so that you appreciate them when they're right, you believe lies so you eventually learn to trust no one but yourself, and sometimes good things fall apart so better things can fall together."
~Marilyn Monroe

"Imperfection is beauty, madness is genius and it's better to be absolutely ridiculous than absolutely boring."
~Marilyn Monroe

"This life is what you make it. No matter what, you're going to mess up sometimes, it's a universal truth. But the good part is you get to decide how you're going to mess it up. Girls will be your friends – they'll act like it anyway. But just remember, some come, some go. The ones that stay with you through everything – they're your true best friends. Don't let go of them. Also remember, sisters make the best friends in the world. As for lovers, well, they'll come and go too. And babe, I hate to say it, most of them – actually pretty much all of them are going to break your heart, but you can't give up because if you give up, you'll never find your soul mate. You'll never find that half who makes you whole and that goes for everything. Just because you fail once, doesn't mean you're gonna fail at everything. Keep trying, hold on, and always, always, always believe in yourself, because if you don't, then who will, sweetie? So keep your head high, keep your chin up, and most importantly, keep smiling, because life's a beautiful thing and there's so much to smile about."

~Marilyn Monroe

"I don't forgive people because I'm weak, I forgive them because I am strong enough to know people make mistakes."

~Marilyn Monroe

"Tomorrow is always fresh, with no mistakes in it."

~Lucy Maud Montgomery

"We should regret our mistakes and learn from them, but never carry them forward into the future with us."

~Lucy Maud Montgomery

"Growing into your future with health and grace and beauty doesn't have to take all your time. It rather requires a dedication to caring for yourself as if you were rare and precious, which you are, and regarding all life around you as equally so, which it is."

~Victoria Moran

"As knowledge increases, wonder deepens."

~Charles Morgan

"The most important kind of freedom is to be what you really are. You trade in your reality for a role. You trade in your sense for an act. You give up your ability to feel, and in exchange, put on a mask. There can't be any large-scale revolution until there's a personal revolution, on an individual level. It's got to happen inside first."

~Jim Morrison

"There is only one success - to be able to spend your life in your own way."

~Christopher Morley

"Until you make peace with who you are, you'll never be content with what you have."

~Doris Mortman

"Life is what we make it. Always has been. Always will be."

~Grandma Moses

"To forgive is the highest, most beautiful form of love. In return, you will receive untold peace and happiness."

~Robert Muller

"We can only learn to love by loving."

~Iris Murdoch

"If you love someone but rarely make yourself available to him or her, that is not true love."

~Thich Nhat Nanh

"Laughter is a part of the human survival kit."

~David Nathan

"The difference between a mountain and a molehill is your perspective."

~Al Neuharth

"Laughter gives us distance. It allows us to step back from an event, deal with it and then move on."

~Bob Newhart

"Confidence is the most important single factor in this game, and no matter how great your natural talent, there is only one way to obtain and sustain it: work."

~Jack Nicklaus

"It's choice -- not chance -- that determines your destiny."

~Jean Nidetch

"A pair of powerful spectacles has sometimes sufficed to cure a person in love."

~Friedrich Nietzsche

"Convictions are more dangerous enemies of truth than lies"

~Friedrich Nietzsche

"He who has a why to live can bear almost any how."

~Friedrich Nietzsche

"A great attitude does much more than turn on the lights in our worlds; it seems to magically connect us to all sorts of serendipitous opportunities that were somehow absent before we changed."

~Earl Nightingale

"The more intensely we feel about an idea or a goal, the more assuredly the idea, buried deep in our subconscious, will direct us along the path to its fulfillment."

~Earl Nightingale

"Life isn't about keeping score. It's not about how many people call you and it's not about who you've dated, are dating, or haven't dated at all. It isn't about who you've kissed, what sport you play, or which girl or guy likes you.

It's not about your shoes or your hair or the color of your skin or where you live or go to school. In fact, it's not about grades, money, clothes, or colleges that accept you.

Life isn't about if you have lots of friends, or if you are alone, and it's not about how accepted or unaccepted you are.

Life just isn't about that. But life is about who you love and who you hurt. It's about how you feel about yourself. It's about trust, happiness, and compassion. It's about sticking up for your friends and replacing inner hate with love. Life is about avoiding jealousy, overcoming ignorance, and building confidence. It's about what you say and what you mean. It's about seeing people for who they are and not what they have.

Most of all, it's about choosing to use your life to touch someone else's in a way that could never have been achieved otherwise. These choices are what life's about."

~Nike Ad

"Age does not protect you from love. But love, to some extent, protects you from age."

~Anais Nin

"Dreams are necessary to life."

~Anais Nin

"Each friend represents a world in us, a world not born until they arrive, and it is only by this meeting that a new world is born."

~Anais Nin

"Life shrinks or expands in proportion to ones courage."

~Anais Nin

"The only abnormality is the incapacity to love."

~Anais Nin

"Throw your dreams into space like a kite, and you do not know what it will bring back, a new life, a new friend, a new love, a new country."

~Anais Nin

"We don't see things as they are, we see them as we are."

~Anais Nin

"A man is not finished when he is defeated. He is finished when he quits."

~Richard M. Nixon

"Let us begin by committing ourselves to the truth to see it like it is, and tell it like it is, to find the truth, to speak the truth, and to live the truth."

~Richard M. Nixon

"We cannot learn from one another until we stop shouting at one another - until we speak quietly enough so that our words can be heard as well as our voices."

~Richard M. Nixon

"Only love heals. Anger, guilt, and fear can only destroy."

~Alyson Noel

"If you want to win, do the ordinary things better than anyone else does - day in and day out."
~Chuck Noll

"Before you criticize someone, you should walk a mile in their shoes. That way, when you criticize them, you are a mile away from them, and you have their shoes."

~Frieda Norris

"Joy does not simply happen to us. We have to choose joy and keep choosing it every day."

~Henri J.M. Nouwen

"The more you find out about the world, the more opportunities there are to laugh at it."

~Bill Nye

"If you're walking down the right path and you're willing to keep walking, eventually you'll make progress."

~Barack Obama

"You may not always have a comfortable life and you will not always be able to solve all of the world's problems at once but don't ever underestimate the importance you can have because history has shown us that courage can be contagious and hope can take on a life of its own."

~Michelle Obama

"A study in the Washington Post says that women have better verbal skills than men. I just want to say to the authors of that study: 'Duh.'"

~Conan O'Brien

"Do the best you can in every task, no matter how unimportant it may seem at the time. No one learns more about a problem than the person at the bottom."

~Sandra Day O'Connor

"To exercise at or near capacity is the best way I know of reaching a true introspective state. If you do it right, it can open all kinds of inner doors."

~Al Oerter

"I've been absolutely terrified every moment of my life and I've never let it keep me from doing a single thing that I wanted to do."

~Georgia O'Keeffe

"A good thing to remember is somebody's got it a lot worse than we do."
~Joel Osteen

"You can be happy where you are."
~Joel Osteen

"Choosing to be positive and having a grateful attitude is going to determine how you're going to live your life."
~Joel Osteen

"Do all you can to make your dreams come true."

~Joel Osteen

"God wants to bless us where we are."

~Joel Osteen

"If you want to rear financial blessings, you have to sow financially."
~Joel Osteen

"When you focus on being a blessing, God makes sure that you are always blessed in abundance."

~Joel Osteen

"The world is a much more beautiful and incredible place than you think, and each of us has a great deal of power to make it more so."

~Oie Osterkamp

"A horse never runs so fast as when he has other horses to catch up and outpace."

~Ovid

"If you want to be loved, be lovable."

~Ovid

"Let love steal in disguised as friendship."

~Ovid

Follow Your Dreams

"Love's dominion, like a kings, admits of no partition."
~Ovid

"Sometimes it's important to work for that pot of gold. But other times it's essential to take time off and to make sure that your most important decision in the day simply consists of choosing which color to slide down on the rainbow."

~Douglas Pagels

"The best way to measure how much you've grown isn't by inches or the number of laps you can now run around the track, or even your grade point average -- though those things are important, to be sure. It's what you've done with your time, how you've chosen to spend your days, and whom you've touched this year. That, to me, is the greatest measure of success."

~R.J. Palacio

"I have learned over the years that when one's mind is made up, this diminishes fear."

~Rosa Parks

"The trouble with most of us is that we would rather be ruined by praise than saved by criticism."

~Norman Vincent Peale

"There are two things a person should never be angry at, what they can help, and what they cannot."

~Plato

"Fortune favors the prepared mind."

~Louis Pasteur

"Show kindness whenever possible. Show it to the people in front of you, the people coming up behind you, and the people with whom you are running neck and neck. It will vastly improve the quality of your own life, the lives of others, and the state of the world."

~Ann Patchett

"A pint of sweat saves a gallon of blood."

~General George S. Patton

"Always do everything you ask of those you command."
~George S. Patton

"I don't measure a man's success by how high he climbs but how high he bounces when he hits bottom."

~George S. Patton

"If everyone is thinking alike, then somebody isn't thinking."
~George S. Patton

"Never tell people how to do things. Tell them what to do and they will surprise you with their ingenuity."
~George S. Patton

"Now if you are going to win any battle you have to do one thing. You have to make the mind run the body. Never let the body tell the mind what to do. The body will always give up.It is always tired morning, noon, and night. But the body is never tired if the mind is not tired. When you were younger the mind could make you dance all night, and the body was never tired... You've always got to make the mind take over and keep going."

~George S. Patton

"If I only had three words of advice, they would be, Tell the Truth. If I got three more words, I'd add, All the Time."

~Randy Pausch

"The best way to have a good idea is to have lots of ideas."

~Linus Pauling

"The cost of not following your heart, is spending the rest of your life … wishing you had."

~J Paulsen

"We cannot change the cards we are dealt, just how we play the hand."

~Randy Pausch

"Love is not a desire for beauty; it is a yearning for completion."

~Octavio Paz

"Believe in yourself! Have faith in your abilities! Without a humble but reasonable confidence in your own powers you cannot be successful or happy."

~Norman Vincent Peale

"Empty pockets never held anyone back. Only empty heads and empty hearts can do that."

~Norman Vincent Peale

"Never talk defeat. Use words like hope, belief, faith, victory."

~Norman Vincent Peale

"The way to happiness: Keep your heart free from hate, your mind from worry. Live simply, expect little, give much. Scatter sunshine, forget yourself, and think of others."

~Norman Vincent Peale

"I know you aren't perfect. But it's a person's imperfections that make them perfect for someone else."

~Stephanie Perkins

"Let our New Year's resolution be this: we will be there for one another as fellow members of humanity, in the finest sense of the word."

~Goran Persson

"Success is focusing the full power of all you are on what you have a burning desire to achieve."

~Wilfred Peterson

"Love is the crowning grace of humanity, the holiest right of the soul, the golden link which binds us to duty and truth, the redeeming principle that chiefly reconciles the heart to life, and is prophetic of eternal good."

~Petrarch

"What is defeat? Nothing but education; nothing but the first step to something better."

~Wendell Phillips

"Action is the foundational key to all success."

~Pablo Picasso

"Art is not the application of a canon of beauty but what the instinct and the brain can conceive beyond any canon. When we love a woman we don't start measuring her limbs."

~Pablo Picasso

"Colors, like features, follow the changes of the emotions."

~Pablo Picasso

"He can who thinks he can, and he can't who thinks he can't."

~Pablo Picasso

"Love is the greatest refreshment in life."

~Pablo Picasso

"There's always going to be bad stuff out there. But here's the amazing thing -- light trumps darkness, every time. You stick a candle into the dark, but you can't stick the dark into the light."

~Jodi Picoult

"Apply yourself both now and in the next life. Without effort, you cannot be prosperous. Though the land be good, you cannot have an abundant crop without cultivation."

~Plato

"Love is the joy of the good, the wonder of the wise, the amazement of the gods; desired by those who have no part in him, and precious to those who have the better part in him."

~Plato

"Those who dream by day are cognizant of many things which escape those who only dream by night."

~Edgar Allan Poe

"Sometimes falling flat on your face allows you to see things from a totally different perspective."

~Linda Poindexter

"The only good luck many great men ever had was being born with the ability and determination to overcome bad luck."

~Channing Pollock

"Freedom consists not in doing what we like, but in having the right to do what we ought."
~Pope John Paul II

Follow Your Dreams

"I think fitting in is highly overrated. I'd rather just fit out... Fitting out means being who you are, even when people insist that you have to change. Fitting out means taking up space, not apologizing for yourself, and not agreeing with those who seek to label you with stereotypes."

~Golda Poretsky

"Ambition is a dream with a V8 engine."

~Elvis Presley

"Love is space and time measured by the heart."

~Marcel Proust

"There can be no peace of mind in love, since the advantage one has secured is never anything but a fresh starting-point for further desires."

~Marcel Proust

"You've gotta dance like there's nobody watching, love like you'll never be hurt, sing like there's nobody listening, and live like it's heaven on earth."

~William W. Purkey

"Sometimes the wrong choices bring us to the right places."

~Nathan Pyle

"It is better wither to be silent, or to say things of more value than silence. Sooner throw a pearl at hazard than an idle or useless word; and do not say a little in many words, but a great deal in a few."

~Pythagoras

"That friendship will not continue to the end which is begun for an end."
~Francis Quareles

"Don't ever confuse the two, your life and your work. That's what I have to say. The second is only part of the first."
~Anna Quindlen

"I would be the most content if my children grew up to be the kind of people who think decorating consists mostly of building enough bookshelves."
~Anna Quindlen

"The only way to get positive feelings about yourself is to take positive actions. Man does not live as he thinks, he thinks as he lives."
~Vaughan Quinn

"Facts are the enemy of truth."
~Don Quixote

"Courage doesn't always roar. Sometimes courage is the quiet voice at the end of the day saying, 'I will try again tomorrow.'"
~Mary Anne Radmacher

"A creative man is motivated by the desire to achieve, not by the desire to beat others."
~Ayn Rand

"Do not let your fire go out, spark by irreplaceable spark in the hopeless swamps of the not quite, the not yet, and the not at all. Do not let the hero in your soul perish in lonely frustration for the life you deserved and have never been able to reach. The world you desire can be won. It exists. It is real. It is possible. It is yours."

~Ayn Rand

"My wish for you is that this life becomes all that you want it to. Your dreams stay big, and your worries stay small. You never need to carry more than you can hold and while you're out there getting where you're getting to, I hope you know somebody loves you, and wants the same things too. This is my wish."

~Rascal Flatts

"When your intention is great enough you will ALWAYS find the time and energy to accomplish your desires. You can state excuses to the contrary, but holding on to your old stories is just another way of wasting precious time."

~James Arthur Ray

"Freedom is never more than one generation away from extinction. We didn't pass it to our children in the bloodstream. It must be fought for, protected, and handed on for them to do the same."
~Ronald Reagan

"There are no easy answers but there are simple answers. We must have the courage to do what we know is morally right."

~Ronald Reagan

"Life's challenges are not supposed to paralyze you, they're supposed to help you discover who you are."
~Bernice J. Reagon

"We must assume every event has significance and contains a message that pertains to our questions. This especially applies to what we used to call bad things. The challenge is to find the silver lining in every event, no matter how negative."

~James Redfield

"When one finds oneself in a hole of one's own making, it is a good time to examine the quality of the workmanship."

~John Renmerde

"Give me a man or woman who has read thousands of books and you give me an interesting companion."

~Anne Rice

"If you think taking care of yourself is selfish, change your mind. If you don't, you're simply ducking your responsibilities."

~Ann Richards

"The possibility for rich relationships exists all around you - you simply have to open your eyes, open your mouth and most importantly, open your heart."

~Cheryl Richardson

"Love consists in this, that two solitudes protect and touch and greet each other."

~Rainer Maria Rilke

"Perhaps all the dragons in our lives are princesses who are only waiting to see us act, just once, with beauty and courage. Perhaps everything that frightens us is, in its deepest essence, something helpless that wants our love."

~Rainer Maria Rilke

"There is no such thing as a weird human being. It's just that some people require more understanding than others."

~Tom Robbins

"A real decision is measured by the fact that you've taken a new action. If there's no action, you haven't truly decided."
~Tony Robbins

"Everybody's got a past. The past does not equal the future unless you live there."

~Tony Robbins

"I challenge you to make your life a masterpiece. I challenge you to join the ranks of those people who live what they teach, who walk their talk."

~Anthony Robbins

"If you do what you've always done, you'll get what you've always gotten."
~Tony Robbins

"If you don't set a baseline standard for what you'll accept in life, you'll find it's easy to slip into behaviors and attitudes or a quality of life that's far below what you deserve."
~Tony Robbins

"If you want to be successful, find someone who has achieved the results you want and copy what they do and you'll achieve the same results."

~Tony Robbins

"It's not the events of our lives that shape us, but our beliefs as to what those events mean."
~Tony Robbins

"Setting goals is the first step in turning the invisible into the visible."
~Tony Robbins

"To effectively communicate, we must realize that we are all different in the way we perceive the world and use this understanding as a guide to our communication with others."
~Tony Robbins

"Winners take imperfect action while losers are still perfecting the plan."
~Tony Robbins

"Nobody can go back a start a new beginning, but anyone can start today and make a new ending."
~Maria Robinson

"The road to happiness lies in two simple principles: find what interests you and that you can do well, and put your whole soul into it -- every bit of energy and ambition and natural ability you have."
~John D. Rockefeller III

"The only person who is educated is the one who has learned how to learn and change."
~Carl Rogers

"We are all here for a spell, get all the good laughs you can. "
~Will Rogers

"Discipline is the bridge between goals and accomplishment."
~Jim Rohn

"Either you run the day or the day runs you."
Jim Rohn

"Happiness is not something you postpone for the future; it is something you design for the present."
~Jim Rohn

"Goals. There's no telling what you can do when you get inspired by them. There's no telling what you can do when you believe in them. There's no telling what will happen when you act upon them."

~Jim Rohn

"Happiness is not something you postpone for the future; it is something you design for the present."
~Jim Rohn

"If you don't design your own life plan, chances are you'll fall into someone else's plan. And guess what they have planned for you? Not much."
~Jim Rohn

"If someone is going down he wrong road, he doesn't need motivation to speed him up, he needs education to turn him around."

~Jim Rohn

"Learn how to be happy with what you have while you pursue all that you want."

~Jim Rohn

"Learning is the beginning of wealth. Learning is the beginning of health. Learning is the beginning of spirituality. Searching and learning is where the miracle process all begins."

~Jim Rohn

"Let others lead small lives, but not you. Let others argue over small things, but not you. Let others cry over small hurts, but not you. Let others leave their future in someone else's hands, but not you."

~Jim Rohn

"Unless you change how you are, you will always have what you've got."

~Jim Rohn

"Work hard at your job and you can make a living. Work hard on yourself and you can make a fortune."

~Jim Rohn

"Beautiful young people are accidents of nature. Beautiful old people are works of art."

~Eleanor Roosevelt

"Do one thing everyday that scares you."

~Eleanor Roosevelt

"Do what you feel in your heart to be right – for you'll be criticized anyway."

~Eleanor Roosevelt

"I learned then that practically no one in the world is entirely bad or entirely good, and that motives are often more important than actions."

~Eleanor Roosevelt

"Learn from the mistakes of others. You can't live long enough to make them all yourself."

~Eleanor Roosevelt

"No one can make you feel inferior without your consent."

~Eleanor Roosevelt

"The future belongs to those who believe in the beauty of their dreams."
~Eleanor Roosevelt

"The future is literally in our hands to mold as we like. But we cannot wait until tomorrow. Tomorrow is now."
~Eleanor Roosevelt

"The giving of love is an education in itself."
~Eleanor Roosevelt

"The purpose of life is to live it, to taste experience to the utmost, to reach out eagerly and without fear for newer and richer experience."
~Eleanor Roosevelt

"With the new day comes new strength and new thoughts."
~Eleanor Roosevelt

"You must do the thing you think you cannot do."
~Eleanor Roosevelt

"Confidence... thrives on honesty, on honor, on the sacredness of obligations, on faithful protection and on unselfish performance. Without them it cannot live."
~Franklin D. Roosevelt

"Do Something. If it works, do more of it. If it doesn't, do something else."
~Franklin D. Roosevelt

"It is common sense to take a method and try it. If it fails, admit it frankly and try another. But above all, try something."
~Franklin D. Roosevelt

"A vote is like a rifle; its usefulness depends upon the character of the user."
~Theodore Roosevelt

"Big jobs usually go to the men who prove their ability to outgrow small ones."
~Theodore Roosevelt

"Do what you can, with what you have, where you are."

~Theodore Roosevelt

"Far and away the best prize that life has to offer is the chance to work hard at work worth doing."
~Theodore Roosevelt

"Far better is it to dare mighty things, to win glorious triumphs, even though checkered by failure... than to rank with those poor spirits who neither enjoy nor suffer much, because they live in a gray twilight that knows not victory nor defeat."
~Theodore Roosevelt

"If you could kick the person in the pants responsible for most of your trouble, you wouldn't sit for a month."
~Theodore Roosevelt

"No man needs sympathy because he has to work, because he has a burden to carry. Far and away the best prize that life offers is the chance to work hard at work worth doing."

~Theodore Roosevelt

"Nobody cares how much you know, until they know how much you care."

~Theodore Roosevelt

"I don't know if anything in nature ever grows exactly the same, but they are always exactly as the way it should be, perfectly itself."
~Bob Ross

"The most beautiful people we have known are those who have known defeat, known suffering, known struggle, known loss, and have found their way out of the depths. These persons have an appreciation, a sensitivity, and an understanding of life that fills them with compassion, gentleness, and a deep loving concern. Beautiful people do not just happen."

~Elizabeth Kubler Ross

"It is impossible to live without failing at something, unless you live so cautiously that you might as well not have lived at all."

~J.K. Rowling

"Never be ashamed! There's some who'll hold it against you, but they're not worth bothering with."

~J. K. Rowling

"I have found that if you love life, life will love you back."

~Arthur Rubinstein

"Winning is great, sure, but if you are really going to do something in life, the secret is learning how to lose. Nobody goes undefeated all the time. If you can pick up after a crushing defeat, and go on to win again, you are going to be a champion someday."

~Wilma Rudolph

"Let us cry for the spilt milk, by all means, if by doing so we learn how to avoid spilling any more. Let us cry for the spilt milk, and remember how, and where, and why, we spilt it.

Much wisdom is learnt through tears, but none by forgetting our lessons."

~Maria Amparo Ruiz de Burton

"When love and skill work together, expect a masterpiece."

~John Ruskin

"The whole problem with the world is that fools and fanatics are always so certain of themselves, and wiser people so full of doubts."

~Bertrand Russell

"Better to be slapped with the truth than kissed with a lie."

~Russian Proverb

"You just can't beat the person who never gives up."

~Babe Ruth

"For small creatures such as we the vastness is bearable only through love."

~Carl Sagan

"Imagination will often carry us to worlds that never were. But without it we go nowhere."
~Carl Sagan

"Wrong is wrong even if everybody is doing it, and right is right even if nobody is doing it."

~St. Augustine

"I am a kind of paranoiac in reverse. I suspect people of plotting to make me happy."

~J.D. Salinger

"Necessity makes even the timid brave."

~Sallust

"The best things happen at the exit ramp of your comfort zone."

~Karen Salmansohn

"The first step to living the life you want is leaving the life you don't want. Taking that first step forward is always the hardest. But then each step forward gets easier and easier. And each step forward gets you closer and closer.

Until eventually, what had once been invisible, starts to be visible. And what had once felt impossible, starts to feel possible."

~Karen Salmansohn

"Think of life as a gigantic ice cream parlor with infinite flavors to taste. Tell yourself the goal of life is to taste as many flavors of experiences as you can. Admittedly, you won't like every flavor. But hey, you don't need to go near that flavor ever again. Instead, indulge in flavors you know you're passionate about! And don't be afraid to taste something that might look funny -- you never know!"

~Karen Salmansohn

"Whenever you're tempted to dwell in the past, repeat this single word: forward. Brainstorm one positive thought and action to use to keep you moving forward. When you're tempted to indulge in a negative, regressive behavior, swap it for one that will move you forward."

~Karen Salmansohn

"A baby is God's opinion that life should go on."

~Carl Sandburg

"Do something you really love in the most adventurous place you can and make sure it helps other people.

~Diane Sawyer

"What we perceive as a failure may simply be our inner being's way of telling us that we are ready to move to a new level of growth."

~Anne Wilson Schaef

"Never cut a tree down in the wintertime. Never make a negative decision in the low time. Never make your most important decisions when you are in your worst moods. Wait. Be patient. The storm will pass. The spring will come."

~Robert H. Schuller

"Tough times never last, but tough people do."
~Robert H. Schuller

"What great thing would you attempt if you knew you could not fail?"
~Robert H. Schuller

"Don't worry about the world coming to an end today. It's already tomorrow in Australia."

~Charles M. Schulz

"The little things, I can obey. But the big things - how we think, what we value - those you must choose yourself. You can't let anyone - or any society - determine those for you."

~Morrie Schwartz

"Do what is right, not what you think the high headquarters wants or what you think will make you look good."

~Norman Schwarzkopf

"He who is brave is free."

~Lucius Annaeus Seneca

"If one does not know to which port one is sailing, no wind is favourable."

~Lucius Annaeus Seneca

"It is the quality rather than the quantity that matters."

~Lucius Annaeus Seneca

"Do you know the difference between education and experience? Education is when you read the fine print; experience is what you get when you don't."
~Pete Seeger

"If things start happening, don't worry, don't stew, just go right along and you'll start happening too."

~Dr. Seuss

"There's no limit to how much you'll know, depending how far beyond zebra you go."

~Dr. Seuss

"Think left and think right and think low and think high. Oh, the thinks you can think up if only you try!"

~Dr. Seuss

"Unless someone like you cares a whole awful lot, nothing is going to get better. It's not."

~Dr. Seuss

"Why fit in, when you were born to stand out."

~Dr. Seuss

"You have brains in your head. You have feet in your shoes.

You can steer yourself any direction you choose. You're on your own. And you know what you know. And YOU are the one who'll decide where to go..."

~Dr. Seuss

"As soon go kindle fire with snow, as seek to quench the fire of love with words."

~William Shakespeare

"Better three hours too soon than a minute too late."

~William Shakespeare

"A life spent making mistakes is not only more honorable, but more useful than a life spent doing nothing."

~George Bernard Shaw

"First love is only a little foolishness and a lot of curiosity."

~George Bernard Shaw

"Life isn't about finding yourself. Life is about creating yourself."
~George Bernard Shaw

"People who say it cannot be done should not interrupt those who are doing it."
~George Bernard Shaw

"The power of accurate observation is frequently called cynicism by those who don't have it."
~George Bernard Shaw

"Write your Sad times in Sand, Write your Good times in Stone."
~George Bernard Shaw

"You see things; and you say, 'Why?' But I dream things that never were; and I say, 'Why not?'"
~George Bernard Shaw

"Ships in harbour are safe, but that's not what ships are built for."
~John Shedd

"Love is a mutual self-giving which ends in self-recover."
~Fulton J. Sheen

"The greatest love story ever told is contained in a little white host."
~Fulton J. Sheen

"The soul's joy lies in doing."
~Percy Bysshe Shelley

"Giving opens the way for receiving."
~Florence Scovel Shinn

"Do it well, finish it properly, and move on."

~Eunice Kennedy Shriver

"If you really want world-class success, decide today to stop caring what other people think and keep your own counsel. Others may or may not have your best interests at heart, but you always will. Calm down and listen to the little voice inside and have the guts to follow it. Trust yourself and know that if you're wrong you have the ability to bounce back. Caring about other people is an asset. Caring about what other people think is a liability."

~Steve Siebold

"Listen to the mustn'ts, child. Listen to the don'ts. Listen to the shouldn'ts, the impossibles, the won'ts. Listen to the never haves, then listen close to me... Anything can happen, child. Anything can be."

~Shel Silverstein

"There is a voice inside of you that whispers all day long, 'I feel this is right for me, I know that this is wrong.' No teacher, preacher, parent, friend or wise man can decide what's right for you -- just listen to the voice that speaks inside."

~Shel Silverstein

"Sometimes love is stronger than a man's convictions."

~Isaac Beshivis Singer

"Take a deep breath, pick yourself up, dust yourself off, and start all over again."

~Frank Sinatra

"Put your heart, mind, and soul into even your smallest acts.

This is the secret of success."

~Swami Sivananda

"Love is but the discovery of ourselves in others, and the delight in the recognition."

~Alexander Smith

"We must seek the loving-kindness of God in all the breadth and open-air of common life."

~George A. Smith

"If we keep our little flame alive, our first feeling of enthusiasm of who we are, without the influence or intervention of others, we will prevail."

~Patti Smith

"Never be afraid to fall apart because it is an opportunity to rebuild yourself the way you wish you had been all along."

~Rae Smith

"It is always sad when someone leaves home, unless they are simply going around the corner and will return in a few minutes with ice-cream sandwiches."
~Lemony Snicket

"Be as you wish to seem."

~Socrates

"Be slow to fall into friendship; but when thou art in, continue firm and constant."

~Socrates

"Beware the barrenness of a busy life."

~Socrates

"Death may be the greatest of all human blessings."

~Socrates

"False words are not only evil in themselves, but they infect the soul with evil."

~Socrates

"From the deepest desires often come the deadliest hate."

~Socrates

"He is richest who is content with the least, for content is the wealth of nature."

~Socrates

"It is not living that matters, but living rightly."

~Socrates

"Let him that would move the world first move himself."

~Socrates

"Not life, but good life, is to be chiefly valued."

~Socrates

"Our prayers should be for blessings in general, for God knows best what is good for us."

~Socrates

"Regard your good name as the richest jewel you can possibly be possessed of -- for credit is like fire; when once you have kindled it you may easily preserve it, but if you once extinguish it, you will find it an arduous task to rekindle it again. The way to gain a good reputation is to endeavor to be what you desire to appear."

~Socrates

"The greatest way to live with honor in this world is to be what we pretend to be."

~Socrates

"The only true wisdom is in knowing you know nothing."
~Socrates

"Wisdom begins in wonder."
~Socrates

"Worthless people live only to eat and drink; people of worth eat and drink only to live."
~Socrates

"A good name is rather to be chosen than riches."
~King Solomon

"A merry heart doeth good like medicine."
~King Solomon

"If you see oppression of the poor, and justice and righteousness trampled in a country, do not be astounded."
~King Solomon

"In the day of prosperity be joyful, but in the day of adversity consider."
~King Solomon

"Kindness and faithfulness keep a king safe, through kindness his throne is made secure."
~King Solomon

"Start with God – the first step in learning is bowing down to God; only fools thumb their noses at such wisdom and learning."
~King Solomon

"Train up a child in the way that he should go: and when he is old, he will not depart from it."

~King Solomon

"Your own soul is nourished when you are kind; it is destroyed when you are cruel."

~King Solomon

"A short saying often contains much wisdom."

~Sophocles

"A soul that is kind and intends justice discovers more than any sophist."

~Sophocles

"All a man's affairs become diseased when he wishes to cure evils by evils."

~Sophocles

"Always desire to learn something useful."
~Sophocles

"I would prefer even to fail with honor than win by cheating."

~Sophocles

"It is terrible to speak well and be wrong."

~Sophocles

"One word frees us of all the weight and pain of life: That word is love."

~Sophocles

"Success is dependent of effort."

~Sophocles

"There is no witness so terrible and no accuser so powerful as conscience which dwells within us."

~Sophocles

"Time alone reveals the just man; but you might discern a bad man in a single day."

~Sophocles

"Who seeks shall find."

~Sophocles

"Wisdom outweighs any wealth."

~Sophocles

"To know what you want, to understand why you're doing it, to dedicate every breath in your body to achieve... If you feel you have something to give, if you feel that your particular talent is worth developing, is worth caring for then there's nothing you can`t achieve."

~Kevin Spacey

"It is impossible to repent of love. The sin of love does not exist."

~Muriel Spark

"I don't keep dreams; they keep me. If not for a dream the only reason to live is to provide for those you created and that only leads to resentment. We must always find a new dream and chase it with a passion or the dying is the living we do each day."

~Andy Spaschak

"You know more than you think you do."

~Benjamin Spock

"I have come to understand that every day is something to cherish."

~Nadine Stair

"If I had my life to live over... I'd dare to make more mistakes next time."
~Nadine Stair

"Ideas are like rabbits. You get a couple and learn how to handle them, and pretty soon you have a dozen."
~John Steinbeck

"It is a common experience that a problem difficult at night is resolved in the morning after the committee of sleep has worked on it."
~John Steinbeck

"A very small degree of hope is sufficient to cause the birth of love."
~Stendhal

"Nothing is so perfectly amusing as a total change of ideas."
~Laurence Sterne

"Laws are never as effective as habits."
~Adlai Stevenson

"A friend is a gift you give yourself."
~Robert Louis Stevenson

"Without an open-minded mind, you can never be a great success."
~Martha Stewart

"Getting over those unexpected hurdles may not be exactly enjoyable, but ultimately I believe that such challenges and the solutions we find give us more confidence. They teach us with common sense and determination we can turn what looks like a disaster into a triumph."
~Martha Stewart

"Be careful the environment you choose for it will shape you; be careful the friends you choose for you will become like them."
~W. Clement Stone

"The future is always beginning now."
~Mark Strand

"Instead of putting others down, try improving yourself instead. The only person you have a right to compete with is you. In the meantime, treat others how you'd like to be treated. One trait that some of the best (communicators) share is empathy. A couple of kind words can not only make a person's day, but earn you a friend and supporter for life.

For the rest of the week, whenever you see someone you want to judge negatively, pay them a compliment instead. See what happens."

~Neil Strauss

"Success is a little like wrestling a gorilla. You don't quit when you are tired -- you quit when the gorilla is tired."

~Robert Strauss

"When a person becomes crystal clear as to exactly what they want to accomplish, and focuses their time and energy on this one goal, any person can move mountains."

~Jimmy Sweeney

"A man should never be ashamed to own that he has been in the wrong, which is but saying... that he is wiser today than yesterday."

~Jonathan Swift

"I wonder what fool it was that first invented kissing."

~Jonathan Swift

"I've always believed no matter how many shots I miss, I'm going to make the next one."

~Jonathan Swift

"If you can't change your fate, change your attitude."
~Amy Tan

"Pour yourself a drink, put on some lipstick, and pull yourself together."
~Elizabeth Taylor

"Success comes in a lot of ways, but it doesn't come with money and it doesn't come with fame. It comes from having a meaning in your life, doing what you love and being passionate about what you do. That's having a life of success. When you have the ability to do what you love, love what you do and have the ability to impact people. That's having a life of success. That's what having a life of meaning is."
~Tim Tebow

"Something I learned early is to not worry about what I can't control... But what I can control is my attitude, my effort, and my focus every single day."
~Tim Tebow

"If I had a flower for every time I thought of you... I could walk through my garden forever."
~Alfred Tennyson

"Be faithful in small things because it is in them that your strength lies."
~Mother Teresa

"Being unwanted, unloved, uncared for, forgotten by everybody, I think that is a much greater hunger, a much greater poverty than the person who has nothing to eat."
~Mother Teresa

"I can do no great things, only small things with great love."

~Mother Teresa

"If you can't feed a hundred people, then feed just one."

~Mother Teresa

"Intense love does not measure, it just gives."

~Mother Teresa

"Kind words can be short and easy to speak, but their echoes are truly endless."

~Mother Teresa

"Let us always meet each other with smile, for the smile is the beginning of love."

~Mother Teresa

"Let us touch the dying, the poor, the lonely and the unwanted according to the graces we have received and let us not be ashamed or slow to do the humble work."

~Mother Teresa

"Life is an opportunity, benefit from it. Life is beauty, admire it. Life is a dream, realize it. Life is a challenge, meet it. Life is a duty, complete it. Life is a game, play it. Life is a promise, fulfill it. Life is sorrow, overcome it. Life is a song, sing it. Life is a struggle, accept it. Life is a tragedy, confront it. Life is an adventure, dare it. Life is luck, make it. Life is too precious, do not destroy it.

Life is life, fight for it."

~Mother Teresa

"Love begins at home, and it is not how much we do...but how much love we put into that action."

~Mother Teresa

"Love begins by taking care of the closest ones – the ones at home."

~Mother Teresa

"Peace begins with a smile."

~Mother Teresa

"People are often unreasonable and self-centered. Forgive them anyway. If you are kind, people may accuse you of ulterior motives. Be kind anyway. If you are honest, people may cheat you. Be honest anyway. If you find happiness, people may be jealous. Be happy anyway. The good you do today may be forgotten tomorrow. Do good anyway. Give the world the best you have and it may never be enough. Give your best anyway."

~Mother Teresa

"Spread love everywhere you go. Let no one ever come to you without leaving happier."

~Mother Teresa

"The poor give us much more than we give them. They're such strong people, living day to day with no food. and they never curse, never complain. We have so much to learn from them."

~Mother Teresa

"We ourselves feel that what we are doing is just a drop in the ocean. But the ocean would be less because of that missing drop."

~Mother Teresa

"Words which do not give the light of Christ increase the darkness."

~Mother Teresa

"It may be the cock that crows but it is the hen that lays the egg."

~Margaret Thatcher

"People think that at the top there isn't much room. They tend to think of it as an Everest. My message is that there is tons of room at the top."
~Margaret Thatcher

"You're worried about how you're going to feel at the end of your life? What about right now? Live. Right this minute. That's where the joy's at."
~Abigail Thomas

"All of us are born for a reason, but all of us don't discover why. Success in life has nothing to do with what you gain in life or accomplish for yourself. It's what you do for others."
~Danny Thomas

Peace is not the absence of conflict but the presence of creative alternatives for responding to conflict - alternatives to passive or aggressive responses, alternatives to violence.
- Dorothy Thompson

"Go confidently in the direction of your dreams. Live the life you've imagined."
~Henry David Thoreau

"Heaven is under our feet as well as over our heads."
~Henry David Thoreau

"If you have built castles in the air, your work need not be lost; that is where they should be. Now put the foundations under them."
~Henry David Thoreau

"It's not what you look at that matters, it's what you see."
~Henry David Thoreau

"Men have become the tools of their tools."
~Henry David Thoreau

"Never look back unless you are planning to go that way."

~Henry David Thoreau

"Things do not change; we change."

~Henry David Thoreau

"We have to learn to be our own best friends because we fall too easily into the trap of being our own worst enemies."

~Roderick Thorp

"For myself, losing is not coming second. It's getting out of the water knowing you could have done better. For myself, I have won every race I've been in."

~Ian Thorpe

"Don't ask what the world needs. Ask what makes you come alive, and go do it. Because what the world needs is people who have come alive."
~Howard Thurman

"Still round the corner there may wait, a new road or a secret gate."

~J. R. R. Tolkien

"If you get the inside right, the outside will fall into place."

~Eckhart Tolle

"Some changes look negative on the surface but you will soon realize that space is being created in your life for something new to emerge."

~Eckhart Tolle

"All, everything that I understand, I understand only because I love."
~Leo Tolstoy

"It is not beauty that endears; it's love that makes us see beauty."

~Leo Tolstoy

"When you love someone, you love the person as they are, and not as you'd like them to be."

~Leo Tolstoy

"Do not let yourselves be discouraged or embittered by the smallness of the success you are likely to achieve in trying to make life better. You certainly would not be able, in a single generation, to create an earthly paradise. Who could expect that? But, if you make life ever so little better, you will have done splendidly, and your lives will have been worthwhile."

~Arnold Toynbee

"All successful people are big dreamers. They imagine what their future could be, ideal in every respect, and then they work every day toward their distant vision, that goal or purpose."

~Brian Tracy

"An average person with average talent, ambition and education, can outstrip the most brilliant genius in our society, if that person has clear, focused goals."
~Brian Tracy

"Decisiveness is a characteristic of high-performing men and women. Almost any decision is better than no decision at all."
~Brian Tracy

"Goals are the fuel in the furnace of achievement."
~Brian Tracy

"If I had to pick the #1 key to success, it would be self-discipline. It is the difference in winning or losing; between greatness and mediocrity."

~Brian Tracy

"I've found that luck is quite predictable. If you want more luck, take more chances. Be more active. Show up more often."
~Brian Tracy

"Issue a blanket pardon. Forgive everyone who has ever hurt you in any way. Forgiveness is a perfectly selfish act. It sets you free from the past."

~Brian Tracy

"Make a game of finding something positive in every situation.

Ninety-five percent of your emotions are determined by how you interpret events to yourself."

~Brian Tracy

"People with clear, written goals, accomplish far more in a shorter period of time than people without them could ever imagine."
~Brian Tracy

"Successful people are always looking for opportunities to help others. Unsuccessful people are always asking, 'What's in it for me?'"
~Brian Tracy

"The more you seek security, the less of it you have. But the more you seek opportunity, the more likely it is that you will achieve the security that you desire."
~Brian Tracy

"Those people who develop the ability to continuously acquire new and better forms of knowledge that they can apply to their work and to their lives will be the movers and shakers in our society for the indefinite future."
~Brian Tracy

"I try to take people one at a time, with all the contradictions and compromises that most of us live with."

~Garry Trudeau

"I have found the best way to give advice to your children is to find out what they want and then advise them to do it."

~Harry S. Truman

"Every great dream begins with a dreamer. Always remember, you have within you the strength, the patience, and the passion to reach for the stars to change the world."

~Harriet Tubman

"The payoff of having a little faith -- that someone in need could truly use your help; that a person you used to keep at arm's length could become a friend -- far outweighs the fear of feeling like a fool."

~Alina Tugend

"Do your little bit of good where you are....it's those little bits of good put together that overwhelm the world."

~Desmond Tutu

"A man cannot be comfortable without his own approval."

~Mark Twain

"Age is an issue of mind over matter. If you don't mind, it doesn't matter."
~Mark Twain

"Courage is resistance to fear, mastery of fear – not absence of fear."

~Mark Twain

"Don't go around saying the world owes you a living. The world owes you nothing. It was here first."

~Mark Twain

"Don't part with your illusions. When they are gone you may still exist, but you have ceased to live."
~Mark Twain

"Drag your thoughts away from your troubles... by the ears, by the heels, or any other way you can manage it."
~Mark Twain

"Each person is born to one possession which outvalues all his others – his last breath."
~Mark Twain

"I have never let my schooling interfere with my education."
~Mark Twain

"If you tell the truth you don't have to remember anything."
~Mark Twain

"It's not the size of the dog in the fight, it's the size of the fight in the dog."
~Mark Twain

"Keep away from people who try to belittle your ambitions. Small people always do that, but the really great ones make you feel that you too, can become great."
~Mark Twain

"Life is short, break the rules. Forgive quickly, kiss slowly.
Love truly. Laugh uncontrollably and never regret anything that makes you smile."
~Mark Twain

"Loyalty to country ALWAYS. Loyalty to government, when it deserves it."
~Mark Twain

"The dictionary is the only place where success comes before work."
~Mark Twain

"It is curious that physical courage should be so common in the world and moral courage so rare."
~ Mark Twain

"Keep away from people who try to belittle your ambitions.
Small people always do that, but the really great ones make you feel that you too can become great."
~Mark Twain

"Some of the worst things in my life never happened."
~Mark Twain

"Two things are infinite: the universe and human stupidity; and I'm not sure about the universe."

~Mark Twain

"When I was a boy of 14, my father was so ignorant I could hardly stand to have the old man around. But when I got to be 21, I was astonished at how much the old man had learned in seven years."
~Mark Twain

"Be a good listener. Your ears will never get you in trouble."

~Frank Tyger

"I'm sixty-five years old. It took me until I was sixty to realize I didn't know everything."

~Steven Tyler

"Drugs will get you out of your own way, but we lived it, and that's dangerous. It can actually turn around on itself and steal your soul, and that's what happened."

~Steven Tyler

"Every life has a measure of sorrow, and sometimes this is what awakens us."

~Steven Tyler

"The things that come to those that wait may be the things left by those that got there first."

~Steven Tyler

"You've reached them, and I've always wanted to reach people. I'm the first one to say I love my fans because they love that I took a chance."

~Steven Tyler

"We need to go back to the way it was 30 years ago, when everybody had Grandma and Grandpa, and we were willing to pass moral judgments about right and wrong."

~Steven Tyler

"When that second airplane hit the building, we all changed. We need to get back to some serious thinking."

~Steven Tyler

"All difficult things have their origin in that which is easy, and great things in that which is small."
~Lao Tzu

"Because of a great love, one is courageous."

~Lao Tzu

"Great acts are made up of small deeds."

~Lao Tzu

"If you look to others for fulfillment, you will never truly be fulfilled. If your happiness depends on money, you will never be happy with yourself. Be content with what you have; rejoice in the way things are. When you realize there is nothing lacking, the whole world belongs to you."

~Lao Tzu

"Knowing others is intelligence; knowing yourself is true wisdom. Mastering others is strength, mastering yourself is true power."
~Lao-Tzu

"Life is a series of natural and spontaneous changes. Don't resist them; that only creates sorrow. Let reality be reality.
Let things flow naturally forward in whatever way they like."
~Lao Tzu

"Nature does not hurry, yet everything is accomplished."
~Lao Tzu

"Silence is a source of great strength."
~Lao Tzu

"The power of intuitive understanding will protect you from harm until the end of your days."
~Lao Tzu

"When I let go of what I am, I become what I might be."
~Lao Tzu

"Nobody grows old merely by living a number of years. We grow old by deserting our ideals. Years may wrinkle the skin, but to give up enthusiasm wrinkles the soul."

~Samuel Ullman

"When you start to really know someone, all his physical characteristics start to disappear. You begin to dwell in his energy, recognize the scent of his skin. You see only the essence of the person, not the shell. That's why you can't fall in love with beauty. You can lust after it, be infatuated by it, want to own it. You can love it with your eyes and body but not your heart. And that's why, when you really connect with a person's inner self, any physical imperfections disappear, become irrelevant."

~Lisa Unger

"Being honest about your feelings is the first chapter in the book of love. Having the courage to follow your heat is second."

~Unknown

"Do something today that your future self will thank you for."

~Unknown

"Don't worry about the people in your past. There's a reason they didn't make it to your future."

~Unknown

"Every day may not be good, but there's something good in every day."

~Unknown

"Everything is a life lesson. Everyone you meet, everything you encounter, etc. They're all part of the learning experience we call 'life.' Never forget to acknowledge the lesson, especially when things don't go your way. If you don't get a job that you wanted or a relationship doesn't work, it only means something better is out there waiting. And the lesson you just learned is the first step towards it."
~Author Unknown

"Forgiveness does not always lead to a healed relationship. Some people are not capable of love, and it might be wise to let them go along with your anger. Wish them well, and let them go their way."

~Unknown

"Immature people always want to win an argument, even at the cost of a relationship. Mature people understand that it's always better to lose an argument and win a relationship."
~Unknown

"Instead of giving myself reasons why I can't, I give myself reasons why I can."

~Unknown

"Just because I laugh a lot, doesn't mean my life is easy.

Just because I have a smile on my face every day, doesn't mean that something is not bothering me. I just choose to move on, and not dwell on all the negatives in my life. Every new moment gives me the chance to renew anew. I choose to be that."

~Unknown

"Kindness is difficult to give away because it keeps coming back to you."
~Unknown

"Life is about trusting your feelings and taking chances, losing and finding happiness, appreciating the memories, learning from the past, and realizing people change."

~Unknown

"Life's problems wouldn't be called "hurdles" if there wasn't a way to get over them."

~Unknown

"Live life and take chances. Believe that everything happens for a reason and don't regret. Love to the fullest and you will find true happiness in life. Realize that things go wrong and people change, but things do go on. Sometimes things weren't meant to be. What is supposed to happen will work its way out."

~Unknown

"Love is not about finding the right person, but creating a right relationship. It's not about how much love you have in the beginning but how much love you build till the end."

~Unknown

"The first to apologize is the bravest, the first to forgive is the strongest, and the first to forget is the happiest."

~Unknown Author

"There comes a time in your life, when you walk away from all the drama and people who create it. You surround yourself with people who make you laugh. Forget the bad, and focus on the good. Love the people who treat you right, pray for the ones who don't. Life is too short to be anything but happy. Falling down is a part of life, getting back up is living."

~Unknown

"Time decides who you meet in life, your heart decides who you want in your life, and your behavior decides who stays in your life."

~Author Unknown

"To the world you may only be one person, but to one person you may be the world."

~Unknown

"Until you commit your goals to paper, you have intentions that are seeds without soil."

~Unknown

"We cannot direct the wind but we can adjust the sails."

~Unknown

"What you do today in important because you are exchanging a day of your life for it."

~Unknown

"When you help someone up a hill, you're that much nearer the top yourself."
~Unknown

"You may only be someone in the world, but to someone else, you may be the world."

~Unknown

"Real difficulties can be overcome. It is only the imaginary ones that are unconquerable. "

~Theodore N. Vail

"If you want children to keep their feet on the ground, put some responsibility on their shoulders."
~Abigail Van Buren

"I am seeking. I am striving. I am in it with all my heart."

~Vincent van Gogh

"If you hear a voice within you say, 'You cannot paint,' then by all means paint, and that voice will be silence."

~Vincent Van Gogh

"As we advance in life it becomes more and more difficult, but in fighting the difficulties the inmost strength of the heart is developed."

~Vincent Van Gogh

"You see, we are here, as far as I can tell, to help each other; our brothers, our sisters, our friends, our enemies. That is to help each other and not hurt each other."

~Stevie Ray Vaughan

"I don't believe you have to be better than everybody else. I believe you have to be better than you ever thought you could be."

~Ken Venturi

"Creativity comes from a conflict of ideas."

~Donatella Versace

"To love and be loved is to feel the sun from both sides."

~David Viscott

"God gave us the gift of life; it is up to us to give ourselves the gift of living well."

~Voltaire

"How pleasant it is for a father to sit at his child's board. It is like an aged man reclining under the shadow of an oak which he has planted."
~Voltaire

"I disapprove of what you say, but I will defend to the death your right to say it."

~Voltaire

"Originality is nothing but judicious imitation."

~Voltaire

"Think for yourselves and let others enjoy the privilege to do so, too."

~Voltaire

"If I accept you as you are, I will make you worse; however if I treat you as though you are what you are capable of becoming, I help you become that."

~Johann Wolfgang Von Goethe

"If you treat an individual as if he were what he ought to be and could be, he will become what he ought to be and could be."

~Johann Wolfgang von Goethe

"Without inspiration the best powers of the mind remain dormant. There is a fuel in us which needs to be ignited with sparks."
~Johann Gottfried Von Herder

"Enjoy the little things in life, for one day you'll look back and realize they were big things."
~Kurt Vonnegut

"The winner's edge is not in a gifted birth, a high IQ, or in talent. The winner's edge is all in the attitude, not aptitude. Attitude is the criterion for success."

~Denis Waitley

"Learn from the past, set vivid, detailed goals for the future, and live in the only moment of time over which you have any control: NOW."

~Denis Waitley

"The deepest secret is that life is not a process of discovery, but a process of creation. You are not discovering yourself, but creating yourself anew. Seek therefore, not to find out Who You Are, but seek to determine Who You Want to Be."

~Neale Donald Walsch

"When you give your children knowledge, you are telling them what to think. When you give your children wisdom, you do not tell them what to know, or what is true, but, rather, how to get to their own truth."

~Neale Donald Walsch

"Everything you own should have value, either because it's functional or beautiful or you just love it."

~Peter Walsh

"You have to ask yourself, 'Does this item or thought or response move me closer to my vision for my best life?' If it does, great. If it doesn't, what is it doing in your life?"

~Peter Walsh

"A cloudy day is no match for a sunny disposition."

~William Arthur Ward

"We can throw stones, complain about them, stumble on them, climb over them, or build with them."

~William Arthur Ward

"When we seek to discover the best in others, we somehow bring out the best in ourselves."

~William Arthur Ward

"Simplicity is making the journey of this life with just baggage enough."

~Charles Dudley Warner

"I have learned that success is to be measured not so much by the position that one has reached in life as by the obstacles which he has overcome while trying to succeed."

~Booker T. Washington

"A slender acquaintance with the world must convince every man that actions, not words, are the true criterion of the attachment of friends."

~George Washington

"Friendship is a plant of slow growth and must undergo and withstand the shocks of adversity before it is entitled to the appellation."
~ George Washington

"I hope I shall possess firmness and virtue enough to maintain what I consider the most enviable of all titles, the character of an honest man."
~George Washington

"Let your heart feel for the afflictions and distress of everyone, and let your hand give in proportion to your purse."

~George Washington

"Things are never quite as scary when you've got a best friend."

~Bill Watterson

"Sometimes when I'm talking, my words can't keep up with my thoughts. I wonder why we think faster than we speak... Probably so we can think twice!"

~Bill Watterson

"The very best thing you can do for the whole world is to make the most of yourself."

~Wallace Wattles

"We must not allow the clock and the calendar to blind us to the fact that each moment of life is a miracle and mystery."

~H. G. Wells

"You only live once, but if you do it right, once is enough."

~Mae West

"You're never too old to become younger."

~Mae West

"Art is not a luxury, but a necessity."

~Rebecca West

"I only know that people call me a feminist whenever I express sentiments that differentiate me from a doormat or a prostitute."

~Rebecca West

"I wonder if we are all wrong about each other, if we are just composing unwritten novels about the people we meet?"

~Rebecca West

"There are two ways of spreading light: to be the candle or the mirror that reflects it."

~Edith Wharton

"Face what you think you believe and you will be surprised."

~William Hale White

"Fill your life with as many moments and experiences of joy and passion as you humanly can. Start with one experience and build on it."

~Marcia Wieder

"It is essential to our well-being, and to our lives, that we play and enjoy life. Every single day do something that makes your heart sing."

~Marcia Wieder

"When we are doing what we love, we don't care about time. For at least at that moment, time doesn't exist and we are truly free."

~Marcia Wieder

"You can change your beliefs so they empower your dreams and desires. Create a strong belief in yourself and what you want."

~Marcia Wieder

"You can come to understand your purpose in life by slowing down and feeling your heart's desires."

~Marcia Wieder

"Willingness is essential in any initiation or in making a dream come true. 'I can't' often means 'I won't.' You can change 'I won't' to 'I will' with will power."

~Marcia Wieder

Follow Your Dreams

"Always continue the climb. It is possible for you to do whatever you choose, if you first get to know who you are and are willing to work with a power that is greater than ourselves to do it."
Ella Wheeler Wilcox

"Be yourself; everyone else is already taken."
~Oscar Wilde

"Experience is one thing you can't get for nothing."
~Oscar Wilde

"My wish isn't to mean everything to everyone but something to someone."
~Oscar Wilde

"Yes: I am a dreamer. For a dreamer is one who can only find his way by moonlight, and his punishment is that he sees the dawn before the rest of the world."
~Oscar Wilde

"Love is not only something you feel, it is something you do."
~David Wilkerson

"Bite off more than you can chew, then chew it."
~Ella Williams

"Life is partly what we make it, and partly what it is made by the friends we choose."
~Tennessee Williams

"This is my living faith, an active faith, a faith of verbs: to question, explore, experiment, experience, walk, run, dance, play, eat, love, learn, dare, taste, touch, smell, listen, speak, write, read, draw, provoke, emote, scream, sin, repent, cry, kneel, pray, bow, rise, stand, look, laugh, cajole, create, confront, confound, walk back, walk forward, circle, hide, and seek."

~Terry Tempest Williams

"You must learn a new way to think before you can master a new way to be."
~Marianne Williamson

"The world is not looking for servants, there are plenty of these, but for masters, men who form their purposes and then carry them out, let the consequences be what they may."

~Woodrow Wilson

"Maturity includes the recognition that no one is going to see anything in us that we don't see in ourselves. Stop waiting for a producer. Produce yourself."
~ Marianne Williamson

"Cheers to a new year and another chance for us to get it right."

~Oprah Winfrey

"Here's what my love affair with quotations has taught me: the more you focus on words that uplift you, the more you embody the ideas contained in those words."

~Oprah Winfrey

"I've come to believe that each of us has a personal calling that's as unique as a fingerprint - and that the best way to succeed is to discover what you love and then find a way to offer it to others in the form of service, working hard, and also allowing the energy of the universe to lead you."

~Oprah Winfrey

"Out with everything you don't need -- the junk, clutter, hang-ups and hurts -- and in with the fresh, fantastic, unencumbered life you've always wanted."

~Oprah Winfrey

"You can take from every experience what it has to offer you.

And you cannot be defeated if you just keep taking one breath followed by another."

~Oprah Winfrey

"The big secret in life is that there is no big secret.

Whatever your goal, you can get there if you're willing to work."

~Oprah Winfrey

"The greatest discovery of all time is that a person can change his future by merely changing his attitude."

~Oprah Winfrey

"Don't underestimate the value of Doing Nothing, of just going along, listening to all the things you can't hear, and not bothering."

~Winnie the Pooh

"If ever there is tomorrow when we're not together... there is something you must always remember. You are braver than you believe, stronger than you seem, and smarter than you think. But the most important thing is, even if we're apart... I'll always be with you."

~Winnie the Pooh

"Defeat is not the worst of failures. Not to have tried is the true failure."
~George Edward Woodberry

"Be more concerned with your character than your reputation, because your character is what you really are, while your reputation is merely what others think you are."

~John Wooden

"Failure is not fatal, but failure to change might be."
~John Wooden

"If you don't have time to do it right, when will you have time to do it over?"
~John Wooden

"It's not so important who starts the game but who finishes it."
~John Wooden

"I know the price of success: dedication, hard work, and an unremitting devotion to the things you want to see happen."
~Frank Lloyd Wright

"The longer I live the more beautiful life becomes. If you foolishly ignore beauty, you will soon find yourself without it. Your life will be impoverished. But if you invest in beauty, it will remain with you all the days of your life."
~Frank Lloyd Wright

"There is no kind of ultimate goal to do something twice as good as anyone else can. It's just to do the job as best you can. If it turns out good, fine. If it doesn't, that's the way it goes."
~Chuck Yeager

"The most successful people are those who are good at plan B."
~James Yorke

"Don't let the worst people get the best of you. Save it for the best people instead."

~Doe Zantamata

"Every storm, no matter how big and strong, passes eventually.

Just know and remember that your spirit is much bigger and stronger than any storm that comes your way, and that all storms will fall apart long before you ever would."

~Doe Zantamata

"Insults are like angry bulls... they can only do damage if you let them in. You can't control what people say, but you can control if you let it bother you. No one's opinion of you is more important than your own."

~Doe Zantamata

"There are better golfers, there are better drivers, there are better swimmers, and there are better cooks. The one thing that no one can ever be better than you at is... being you. Just be you. There's no one more qualified for the job."

~Doe Zantamata

"When things just don't work out as good as you really thought they would... It's not rotten, it's not over, it's not finished, or the end. All it means is something better is waiting for you around the bend."

~Doe Zantamata

"You have to accept things in order to be happy. One of the biggest things you have to accept is that if you're not happy, it doesn't have to be that way... but you, and only you, have the power to change your life for the better."

~Doe Zantamata

"Art is making something out of nothing and selling it."
~Frank Zappa

"Communism doesn't work because people like to own stuff."
~Frank Zappa

"Everybody believes in something and everybody, by virtue of the fact that they believe in something, uses that something to support their own existence."
~Frank Zappa

"Don't ever regret anything because regretting means wanting to forget every moment. Every moment is what makes you who you are today, every moment spent in regret is a moment wasted.
Don't waste your moments in life, you never know when you'll stop waking up."
~Maryam Zarei

"A goal, properly set, is halfway reached."
~Zig Ziglar

"Building a better you is the first step to building a better America."
~Zig Ziglar

"Every choice you make has an end result."
~Zig Ziglar

"Expect the best. Prepare for the worst. Capitalize on what comes."
~Zig Ziglar

"Failure is a detour, not a dead-end street."
~Zig Ziglar

"I believe that being successful means having a balance of success stories across the many areas of your life. You can't truly be considered successful in your business life if your home life is in shambles."

~Zig Ziglar

"If God would have wanted us to live in a permissive society He would have given us Ten Suggestions and not Ten Commandments."

~Zig Ziglar

"If you can dream it, then you can achieve it. You will get all you want in life if you help enough other people get want they want."

~Zig Ziglar

"If you don't see yourself as a winner, then you cannot perform as a winner."

~Zig Ziglar

"If you go looking for a friend, you're going to find they're very scarce. If you go out to be a friend, you'll find them everywhere."

~Zig Ziglar

"If you learn from defeat, you haven't really lost."

~Zig Ziglar

"If you want to reach a goal, you must "see the reaching" in your own mind before you actually arrive at your goal."

~Zig Ziglar

"It was character that got us out of bed, commitment that moved us into action, and discipline that enabled us to follow through."

~Zig Ziglar

"It's not what you've got, it's what you use that makes a difference."

~Zig Ziglar

"Little men with little minds and little imaginations go through life in little ruts, smugly resisting all changes which would jar their little worlds."
~Zig Ziglar

"Many marriages would be better if the husband and the wife clearly understood that they are on the same side."
~Zig Ziglar

"Money isn't the most important thing in life, but it's reasonably close to oxygen on the 'gotta have it' scale."
~Zig Ziglar

"Positive thinking will let you do everything better than negative thinking will."
~Zig Ziglar

"Regardless of your lot in life,you can still build something beautiful on it "
~Zig Ziglar

"The more you recognize and express gratitude for the things you have, the more things you will have to express gratitude for."
~Zig Ziglar

"You never know when a moment and a few sincere words can have an impact on a life."
~Zig Ziglar

This next section contains my favorite quotes, and if you keep in mind that I'm an author, you will understand why...

"Of all diversions in life, there is none so proper as the reading of useful and entertaining authors."

~Joseph Addison

"The act of writing is an act of optimism. You would not take the trouble to do it if you felt that it didn't matter."

~Edward Albee

"Effective readers, even at their earliest levels, read in five to seven word phrases rather than word-by-word."

~Richard L. Allington

"Writing is hard, even for authors who do it all the time."

~Roger Angell

"Over time I have learned I am at my best around books."

~Maya Angelou

"A book is like a garden carried in the pocket."

~Arab Proverb

"If the doctor told me I had six minutes to live, I'd type a little faster. "

~Isaac Asimov

"I write for the same reason I breathe - because if I didn't, I would die."

~Isaac Asimov

"The world is a book and those who do not travel read only one page."

~Saint Augustine of Hippo

"The only thing I was fit for was to be a writer, and this notion rested solely on my suspicion that I would never be fit for real work, and that writing didn't require any."

~Russell Baker

"The writer seems to want everybody, and at the same time, needs no one at all."

~James Arthur Baldwin

"It took me fifteen years to discover I had no talent for writing, but I couldn't give it up because by that time I was too famous."

~Robert Benchley

"Successful writers learn at last what they should learn at first, -- to be intelligently simple."

~Josh Billings

"I have always imagined that Paradise will be a kind of library."

~Jorge Luis Borges

"Characters are not created by writers. They pre-exist and have to be found."

~Elizabeth Bowen

"Libraries raised me."

~Ray Bradbury

"Quantity produces quality. If you only write a few things, you're doomed."

~Ray Bradbury

"I don't think it is possible to give tips for finding one's voice; it's one of those things for which there aren't really any tricks or shortcuts, or even any advice that necessarily translates from writer to writer. All I can tell you is to write as much as possible."

~Poppy Z. Brite

"No man should ever publish a book until he has first read it to a woman."

~Van Wyck Brooks

"I'm just going to write because I cannot help it."

~Charlotte Bronte

"If you write one story, it may be bad; if you write a hundred, you have the odds in your favor."

~Edgar Rice Burroughs

"Every word written is a victory against death."

~Michel Butor

"Metaphors have a way of holding the most truth in the least space."

~Orson Scott Card

"I was born with a reading list I will never finish."

~Maud Casey

"The faster I write the better my output. If I'm going slow, I'm in trouble. It means I'm pushing the words instead of being pulled by them."

~Raymond Chandler

"A book is like a garden carried in the pocket. "

~Chinese Proverb

"I've always believed in writing without a collaborator, because when two people are writing the same book, each believes he gets all the worries and only half the royalties."

~Agatha Christie

"A home without books is a body without soul."

~Marcus Tullius Cicero

"The difference between fiction and reality? Fiction has to make sense."

~Tom Clancy

"Reading gives us some place to go when we have to stay where we are."

~Mason Cooley

"Whatever the cost of our libraries, the price is cheap compared to that of an ignorant nation."

~Walter Cronkite

"Most writers write faster than publishers can write checks."

~Richard Curtis

"Life is what happens to a writer between drafts."

~Damon (aka Dennis R. Miller)

"I believe that in a good collaboration, the authors bring their strengths to the story; one author's strength cancels the other author's weakness, and back and forth it goes."

~Jack Dann

"Someday I hope to write a book where the royalties will pay for the copies I give away."

~Clarence Darrow

"There is more treasure in books than in all the pirate's loot on Treasure Island."

~Walt Disney

"Writing is a socially acceptable form of schizophrenia."

~E.L. Doctorow

"Writing is turning one's worst moments into money."

~J.P. Donleavy

"Never judge a book by its movie."

~J.W. Eagan

"Our high respect for a well read person is praise enough for literature."

~T.S. Eliot

"Some editors are failed writers, but so are most writers."

~T.S. Eliot

"Books are the quietest and most constant of friends; they are the most accessible and wisest of counselors, and the most patient of teachers."

~Charles William Eliot

"People on the outside think there's something magical about writing, that you go up in the attic at midnight and cast the bones and come down in the morning with a story, but it isn't like that. You sit in back of the typewriter and you work, and that's all there is to it."

~Harlan Ellison

"A man is known by the books he reads."

~Ralph Waldo Emerson

"For every minute you are angry you lose sixty seconds of happiness."

~Ralph Waldo Emerson

"In the highest civilization, the book is still the highest delight."

~Ralph Waldo Emerson

"If you wish to be a writer, write."

~Epictetus

"Write your first draft with your heart. Re-write with your head."

~From the movie "Finding Forrester"

Follow Your Dreams

"If you do not have time to read, then you do not have time to be an author."

~Ken Follett

"You can't say, I won't write today because that excuse will extend into several days, then several months, then... you are not a writer anymore, just someone who dreams about being a writer."

~Dorothy C. Fontana

"For someone like me, it is a very strange habit to write in a diary. Not only that I have never written before, but it strikes me that later neither I, nor anyone else, will care for the outpouring of a thirteen year old schoolgirl."

~Anne Frank

"I want to write, but more than that, I want to bring out all kinds of things that lie buried deep in my heart."

~Anne Frank

"Either write something worth reading or do something worth writing."

~Benjamin Franklin

"I write to find out what I didn't know I knew."

~Robert Frost

"Today a reader, tomorrow a leader."

~Margaret Fuller

"The most beautiful things are those that madness prompts and reason writes."

~ André Gide

"We write because we believe the human spirit cannot be tamed and should not be trained."

~Nikki Giovanni

"A story should have a beginning, a middle, and an end... but not necessarily in that order. "

~Jean Luc Godard

"A synonym is a word you use when you can't spell the other one."

~Baltasar Gracian

"Whether you are inspired or not, the only way to unlock your creativity, is to start writing."

~Jane Green

"Writing's still the most difficult job I've ever had—but it's worth it."

~John Grisham

"Writing is physical work. It's sweaty work. You just can't will yourself to become a good writer. You really have to work at it."

~Will Haygood

"Reading is sometimes an ingenious device for avoiding thought."

~Arthur Helps

"All you have to do is write one true sentence. Write the truest sentence that you know."

~Ernest Hemingway

"I write one page of masterpiece to ninety-one pages of sh*t. I try to put the sh*t in the wastebasket."

~Ernest Hemingway

"There is nothing to writing. All you do is sit down at a typewriter and bleed."

~Ernest Hemingway

"Write drunk. Edit sober."

~Ernest Hemingway

"To be a writer is to sit down at one's desk in the chill portion of every day, and to write; not waiting for the little jet of the blue flame of genius to start from the breastbone – just plain going at it, in pain and delight. To be a writer is to throw away a great deal, not to be satisfied, to type again, and then again, and once more, and over and over...."

Follow Your Dreams

~John Hersey

"Books may well be the only true magic."
~Alice Hoffman

"The old books look out from the shelves, and I seem to read on their backs something besides their titles; a kind of solemn greeting."
~Holmes

"This will never be a more civilized country until we expend more money for books than we do for chewing gum."
~Elbert Hubbard

"Writers write the things they think other folks think they think."
~Elbert Hubbard

"An artist must be free to choose what he does, certainly, but he must also never be afraid to do what he might choose."
~Langston Hughes

"Only a person with a best seller mind can write best sellers."
~Aldous Huxley

"A writer never has a vacation. For a writer life consists of either writing or thinking about writing."
~Eugene Ionesco

"What doesn't kill us, makes us writers."
~Sherry Isaac

"A man will turn over half a library to make one book."
~Samuel Johnson

"A writer only begins a book. A reader finishes it."

~Samuel Johnson

"The two most engaging powers of an author are to make new things familiar and familiar things new."

~Samuel Johnson

"There is nothing so dangerous to an author as silence."

~Samuel Johnson

"Good novels are not written, they are rewritten. Great novels are diamonds mined from layers of rewrites."

~Andre Jute

"Being a writer is like having homework every night for the rest of your life."

~Lawrence Kasdan

"I am a part of all I have read."

~John Kieran

"I am crazy. I have delusions and visions. I write them down and people pay me to read them."

~Stephen King, Lisey's Story

"If you want to be a writer, you must do two things above all others: read a lot and write a lot."

~Stephen King

"Writing isn't about making money, getting famous, getting dates, getting laid, or making friends. In the end, it's about enriching the lives of those who will read your work, and enriching your own life, as well. It's about getting up, getting well, and getting over. Getting happy, okay? Getting happy."

~Stephen King

"What an author says in the morning, will determine the rest of their day. What an author says to others, will determine their image. What an author says in their books, will determine their future."

Follow Your Dreams

~Ron Knight

"Fiction is about stuff that's screwed up."
~Nancy Kress

"The novelist's ambition is not to do something better than his predecessors, but to see what they did not see, say what they did not say."
~Milan Kundera

"Asking a writer what he thinks about critics is like asking a lamp post how it feels about dogs."
~Ann Landers

"Writing is a fairly lonely business, unless you invite people in to watch you do it, which is often distracting and then you have to ask them to leave."
~Marc Lawrence

"The story is not in the plot but in the telling."
~Ursula K. LeGuin

"To be a successful fiction writer you have to write well, write a lot ... and let 'em know you've written it! Then rinse and repeat."
~Gerard de Marigny

"If you want to get rich from writing, write the sort of thing that's read by persons who move their lips when they're reading to themselves."
~Don Marquis

"Go after your dream, no matter how unattainable others think it is."
~Linda Mastandrea

"If you are meant to be a writer, it will work itself out."
~Robin McKinley

"Outside of a dog, a book is man's best friend. Inside of a dog it's too dark to read."

~Groucho Marx

"All the words I use in my stories can be found in the dictionary; it's just a matter of arranging them in the right sentences."

~W. Somerset Maugham

"I often think how much easier life would have been for me and how much time I would have saved if I had known the alphabet. I can never tell where I and J stand without saying G, H to myself first."

~W. Somerset Maugham

"I would sooner read a time-table or a catalogue than nothing at all. They are much more entertaining than half the novels that are written."

~W. Somerset Maugham

"It is unsafe to take your reader for more of a fool than he is."

~W. Somerset Maugham

"It's very hard to be a gentleman and a writer."

~W. Somerset Maugham

"The crown of literature is poetry."

~W. Somerset Maugham

"The best style is the style you don't notice."

~W. Somerset Maugham

"The great American novel has not only already been written, it has already been rejected."

~W. Somerset Maugham

"The trouble with young writers is that they are all in their sixties."

~W. Somerset Maugham

"The writer is more concerned to know than to judge."

~W. Somerset Maugham

"The writer of prose can only step aside when the poet passes."

~W. Somerset Maugham

"There are three rules for writing a novel. Unfortunately, no one knows what they are."

~W. Somerset Maugham

"Things were easier for the old novelists who saw people all of a piece. Speaking generally, their heroes were good through and through, their villains wholly bad."

~W. Somerset Maugham

"To acquire the habit of reading is to construct for yourself a refuge from almost all the miseries of life."

~W. Somerset Maugham

"We do not write because we want to; we write because we have to."

~W. Somerset Maugham

"When I read a book I seem to read it with my eyes only, but now and then I come across a passage, perhaps only a phrase, which has a meaning for me, and it becomes part of me."

~W. Somerset Maugham

"Writing is the supreme solace."

~W. Somerset Maugham

"Best advice on writing I've ever received. Finish."

~Peter Mayle

"To produce a mighty book, you must choose a mighty theme."

~Herman Melville

"Writing is the hardest way to earn a living, with the possible exception of wrestling alligators."

~Olin Miller

"If there's a book you really want to read, but it hasn't been written yet, then you must write it."

~Toni Morrison

"If you only read the books that everyone else is reading, you can only think what everyone else is thinking."

~Haruki Murakami

"We write to taste life twice, in the moment and in retrospection."

~Anais Nin

"If you want to write for yourself, get a diary. If you want to write for a few friends, get a blog. If you want to write for others...become an author."

~James Patterson

"It is not enough to simply teach children to read; we have to give them something worth reading."

~Katherine Patterson

"Nothing stinks like a pile of unpublished writing."

~Sylvia Plath

"Always read something that makes you look good if you die in the middle of it."

~P.J. O'Rourke

"If we had to say what writing is, we would describe it essentially as an act of courage."

~Cynthia Ozick

"A word is not the same with one writer as with another. One tears it from his guts. The other pulls it out of this overcoat pocket."

~Charles Peguy

"I divide readers into two classes: Those who read to remember and those who read to forget."

~William Phelps

"When something can be read without effort, great effort has gone into its writing."

~Enrique Jardiel Poncela

"There's no such thing as writers block. That was invented by people in California who couldn't write."

~Terry Pratchett

"Writing is a way of talking without being interrupted."

~Jules Renard

"Writing is an occupation in which you have to keep proving your talent to those who have none."

~Jules Renard

"The only reason for being a professional writer is that you just can't help it."

~Leo Rosten

"I always read. You know how sharks have to keep swimming or they die? I'm like that. If I stop reading, I die."

~Patrick Rothfuss

"The trade of authorship is a violent and indestructible obsession."

~George Sand

"For me, reading and writing horror is about eating my own shadow, so it won't eat me."

~Harry Shannon

"It is better to write a bad first draft than to write no first draft at all."

~Will Shetterly

"Wicked people never have time for reading. It's one of the reasons for their wickedness."

~Lemony Snicket

"The first chapter sells the book; the last chapter sells the next book."

~Mickey Spillane

"Writing is the only thing that, when I do it, I don't feel I should be doing something else."

~Gloria Steinem

"Being a writer is like standing naked in the High Street hoping people won't find you ridiculous."

~Graham Storrs

"Every writer must acknowledge that he has given himself a life sentence in solitary confinement."

~Peter Straub

"You know you've read a good book when you turn the last page and feel a little as if you have lost a friend."

~Paul Sweeney

"The only way to learn how to write is to write."

~Peggy Teeters

Follow Your Dreams

"Books are the treasured wealth of the world and the fit inheritance of generations and nations."

~Henry David Thoreau

"Books must be read as deliberately and reservedly as they are written."

~Henry David Thoreau

"There is no way of writing well and also of writing easily."

~Anthony Trollope

"Not all readers are leaders, but all leaders are readers."

~Harry S. Truman

"Good friends, good books, and a sleepy conscience; this is the ideal life."

~Mark Twain

"How often we recall with regret that Napoleon once shot at a magazine editor and missed him and killed a publisher. But we remember with charity that his intentions were good."

~Mark Twain

"In a good bookroom you feel in some mysterious way that you are absorbing the wisdom contained in all the books through your skin, without even opening them."

~Mark Twain

"Substitute "damn" every time you're inclined to write "very;" your editor will delete it and the writing will be just as it should be."

~Mark Twain

"It usually takes more than three weeks to prepare a good impromptu speech."

~Mark Twain

"The difference between the almost right word and the right word is really a large matter – it's the difference between the lightning bug and the lightning."

~Mark Twain

"The man who does not read good books has no advantage over the man who can't read."

~Mark Twain

"Writing is easy. All you have to do is cross out the wrong words."

~Mark Twain

"If I'm not in the middle of a literary project, I'm utterly lost, unhappy, and distressed. As soon as I get started, I calm down."

~Kaari Utrio

"Some writers take to drink, others take to audiences."

~Gore Vidal

"Let us read and let us dance – two amusements that will never do any harm to the world."

~Voltaire

"When ideas fail, a word comes to save the situation."

~Johann Wolfgang Von Goethe

"You cannot be a good writer of serious fiction if you are not depressed."

~Kurt Vonnegut

"Just how difficult it is to write biography can be reckoned by anybody who sits down and considers just how many people know the real truth about his or her love affairs."

~Rebecca West

"Writing has nothing to do with communication between person and person, only with communication between different parts of a person's mind."

~Rebecca West

"I would hurl words into this darkness and wait for an echo, and if an echo sounded, no matter how faintly, I would send other words to tell, to march, to fight, to create a sense of hunger for life that gnaws in us all."

~Richard Wright

"I'm writing a book. I've got the page numbers done."

~Steven Wright

www.ingramcontent.com/pod-product-compliance
Lightning Source LLC
Chambersburg PA
CBHW020412290526
45785CB00002B/521

9781300818687